*My* Quest
*For* Beauty

*By the same author*

LOVE AND WILL
THE MEANING OF ANXIETY
MAN'S SEARCH FOR HIMSELF
POWER AND INNOCENCE
THE COURAGE TO CREATE
PSYCHOLOGY & THE HUMAN DILEMMA
FREEDOM AND DESTINY
THE DISCOVERY OF BEING

# *My* Quest For Beauty,

## ROLLO MAY

—————— SAYBROOK ——————

San Francisco                    Dallas                    New York

Quotations from copyrighted poetry and prose are noted in an "Acknowledgments" section at the end of this volume.

Copyright © 1985 by Rollo May

Designed by Don May
Library of Congress Cataloguing in Publication Data

May, Rollo 1909–
    My quest for beauty

        1. Art—Psychology.  I. Title.
N71.M29   1985        701'.1'5        85-61687
ISBN 0-933071-01-9

Saybrook Publishing Company
3518 Armstrong Avenue, Dallas, TX 75205
Printed in the United States of America
Distributed by W.W. Norton & Company
500 Fifth Avenue
New York, New York 10110

# CONTENTS

# PART III

# PART IV

## List of Illustrations

# FOREWORD

This book begins with my experiences as a young man in Greece, which were the origin of my interest in beauty and in art. The travels those summers among the peasant villages of central Europe with a group of artists studying and drawing peasant art gave concrete form to my newly born concerns.

The second part deals with a description of the holy mountain of Athos, in Greece, followed by my expression in fiction of the relation between love and beauty and death. Then some paintings of my own are presented, with the hope that they will express directly some of the things we are talking about. My firm belief is that one paints, as one writes, not out of a theory but out of the vividness of an experience, and I hope the paintings illustrate this. There is a surprisingly close parallel between art and psychotherapy, and in my life they both came out of the same source. In each a new form is born not out of ideas but out of the intensity of experiences.

Rational thoughts follow to anchor theoretically the truths that already have grasped us as a vision. Hence the last chapters deal with the theory of beauty and the art which is its voice.

This book would literally not have been written except for the imagination and persuasion of Pat Howell,

President of Saybrook Publishing Company, who proposed to me, gently but firmly, to allow some of my paintings and drawings be put into print. I take pleasure in acknowledging his part in launching me into a project which has proved as exciting and absorbing as anything I have ever attempted.

# PART · I

R. M.

# CHAPTER I

## Poppies IN Greece

*To burn always with this hard, gemlike flame,*
*to maintain this ecstasy, is success in life.*
*Of such wisdom, the poetic passion,*
*the desire of beauty, the love of art*
*for its own sake, has most.*

*For art comes to you proposing frankly*
*to give nothing but the highest quality*
*to your moments as they pass,*
*and simply for those moments' sake.*

WALTER PATER

3

*I*

Y DEVOTION to beauty and to art began when I was twenty-one and in my second year of teaching in Greece. On graduating from Oberlin, I had agreed to go out as a tutor in English for three years at Anatolia College, in Saloniki, Greece. The name of the college derives from Anatolia, a section in eastern Turkey, from which the older American teachers had also come, each with his or her horrendous story of persecution to tell.

In 1922, the Turks drove the Greeks and the Armenians in a great forced migration of hundreds of miles from Anatolia to the Aegean Sea, and a hundred thousand men, women, and children were literally driven into the Aegean Sea. Most of them were rescued by British war ships standing off shore. These refugees were dumped in Saloniki, and they now made up one third of the city's population. Their college came along with them, so to speak, and began operating in Saloniki in a British casino and several other buildings left over from World War I. The adjacent quadrangle which had been used by the British soldiers now became a boys' dormitory.

Saloniki—the Thessalonika to which St. Paul wrote a letter in the New Testament—is the second largest city in Greece, and is in the northern part of the country on the shores of the Aegean. There were only a handful of American teachers in the college, most of whom had been missionaries in the college when it was in eastern Turkey. In my classes were boys named after the heroes of ancient Greece—Platon, Aristoteles, Socraton, Agamemnonos. The boys were effusive, lovable, emotionally changeable. It was a case of an immediate love affair between the students and myself, but I was later to learn how unstable such adoration could be.

During that first year I went down occasionally to look at the ruins of Byzantine churches in the ancient part of Saloniki, and to watch the barques sailing in from Asia Minor, their decks loaded high with oranges. I was unanimously elected advisor to the third Form in our college. All this seemed to make my first year happy enough. But as the year went on I found that my habits and principles, coming from a typical small-town, midwestern childhood, such as hard work, fidelity, honesty and so on, stood by me less and less as the year progressed.

In the second year I found myself getting very lonely. We few Americans took our meals together (when not on duty with the boys in the quadrangle) and we soon

A street-corner, Saloniki
April, '33

RM

became so well known to each other that there was
nothing left to talk about. Two new young American
men had come out to the college, and the boys in the
school found these new teachers to lavish their incon-
stant affection and charm upon.

I worked harder and harder but it did not assuage my
loneliness. I noticed, furthermore, that the harder I
worked the less effective I was as a teacher. While the
wonders of ancient Greece interested me tremendously,
the occasional trips to Athens and Delphi did not com-
pensate for the loneliness of this circle in which I seemed
trapped.

Finally in the spring of that second year I had what
is called, euphemistically, a nervous breakdown. Which
meant simply that the rules, principles, values by which
I used to work and live simply did not suffice anymore.
I got so completely fatigued that I had to go to bed for
two weeks to get enough energy to continue my teaching. I had learned enough psychology at college to know
that these symptoms meant that something was wrong
with my whole way of life. I had to find some new goals
and purposes for my living and to relinquish my moral-
istic, somewhat rigid way of existence. In the United
States nowadays I would have gone to a therapist. But
then, in 1931, I was in a psychologically primitive culture where only a few people spoke my language. What
to do?

During these two weeks a friendly couple, who were
regular teachers at the college, took me up to their house
to rest. This couple had survived the mass exodus from
Turkey and now lived in the one new house built at
the site a mile up the hill where the college planned
to erect its new buildings when the money became

available. They were honest, warm human beings who talked with me at length when I wanted to talk.

At eleven o'clock one night in March, after a long talk with these friends, I started out walking up the road toward Mt. Hortiati, a relatively large mountain about ten miles away. My hosts asked me where I was going but I did not know, and they trusted me enough not to interfere. It was raining when I started out in the night, and as I got higher up the mountain, the rain changed to snow and my clothes froze to me. But I kept going steadily, concerned only with this inner turmoil in my mind and with a certain peace that at least now I was doing something, taking some steps, though I was not sure where. After about six hours in the darkness, when I had reached a wide plateau near the top of the mountain, I heard the barking of wolves across the plateau. I had been aware that there were a number of wolves in this mountain. I could faintly see their dim forms against the grey snow. They came dashing up to me, ran around me a few times, but I was so absorbed in my inner thoughts that I paid no attention to them. After circling me several times they departed, leaping across the snow and ice of the plateau.

It was just dawn when I arrived at the little village of Hortiati, made up of the huts of perhaps a hundred peasants who obviously would speak no English. The inhabitants herded sheep during the summer and spring and autumn, and during the winter such village women had nothing to do except gather firewood on the mountain, and the men would while away the winter days sitting around the stove in the one café in the little village.

I woke up the café-owner and arranged in my halting

Greek to rent his one room upstairs. The room had a cot but only one old blanket. I took off my frozen clothes and pulled the rug up over me to get warm, and then went to sleep. At noon I got up and made my way downstairs to sit among the twelve or fifteen men who had gathered around the stove in the café. They were mostly peasants and they went on talking, acting friendly toward me but paying little attention.

One of the men took out some little fish like sardines, which he put directly on top of the stove, and when they were a little burned the men pried them off the iron and ate them—a villager's *hors d'oeuvres*. I sat as near the stove as I could to keep warm.

I spent the hours writing on the backs of laundry slips I found in my coat pocket. I was doing a primitive kind of self-analysis, trying to get some perspective, to make some sense of my distraught life, and to find some reliable direction. My loquacious companions soon became curious, and finally they could refrain no longer from asking me what I was doing.

One spoke out, *"Ti graphité?"* which means, "What do you write?" I knew they would not understand if I talked about philosophy, and furthermore it wasn't quite true that I was writing that anyway.

So I answered in my halting Greek, "I write, *what is life?*"

They all leaned back with guffaws of laughter. One of them spoke out, "That's easy! If you have bread you eat, if you do not have bread you die."

I could understand that that might work for them, but it scarcely satisfied the agitation and ache in my own heart. So I continued to pursue my silent questions against this friendly background of Greek chatter.

After two days and two nights I started back down the mountain again. I had a few more days to spend with my friends before going back to teaching, and during this time I walked mostly around the surrounding hills. Ascending one hill I found myself suddenly knee-deep in a field of wild poppies covering the whole hillside. It was a gorgeous sight: brilliantly crimson and scarlet, the poppies were lovely forms as they bent delicately in one direction and then another. Their perfect movements together seemed like children in a ballet, perhaps the "Nutcracker Suite" at Christmas time. I stood there, intoxicated, wholly capitivated by this sight. Wordsworth's words came into my mind.

> I wandered lonely as a cloud
> That floats on high o'er vales and hills,
> When all at once I saw a crowd,
> A host of golden daffodils. . . .
>
> Ten thousand saw I at a glance,
> Tossing their heads in spritely dance.

My poppies in their dance were swaying in unison and bowing in the slight breeze, each of them having a miraculous perfection of beauty in itself. When they nodded toward me they presented their yellow-black centers, and when they nodded away they then seemed a fiery scarlet.

I thought how good it would be to sit among these flowers and draw their forms so that I would never forget them. So I went back to the house and borrowed a pencil and pad and came out to kneel among the poppies to sketch them. They made an imprint on my mind that seems as vivid today as it was then.

This is the drawing that I did that sunny morning:

R.M.

Poppies, drawn at "White House,"
May 22, '32

I realized that I had not listened to my inner voice, which had tried to talk to me about beauty. I had been too hard-working, too "principled" to spend time merely looking at flowers! It seems it had taken a collapse of my whole former way of life for this voice to make itself heard. This inner voice hereafter would always be redolent with the slight perfume that covered the hillside that morning. It is amazing how true Wordsworth's lines were for me:

> For oft, when on my couch I lie
>     In vacant or in pensive mood,
> They flash upon that inward eye
>     Which is the bliss of solitude;
> And then my heart with pleasure fills,
> And dances with the daffodils.

At the beginning of the summer vacation in June, I found myself enrolled in Alfred Adler's seminar at Semmering, a resort in the mountains above Vienna. Contrary to my previous careful, somewhat compulsive planning, I had made no plans for that summer; I was a kind of hippie several decades before such carefree life came into vogue. In an hour between Adler's lectures, I was making a sketch when an American woman stopped to watch me. She inquired about my interest in art. I learned that she was the director of the International School of Art, a group of seventeen or eighteen American artists who were to gather in a week and spend the summer studying peasant art in the villages of Central Europe. She invited me to join the group, and since I did not have the money to pay the regular fees, I went along on a kind of job-scholarship.

The group met first in Vienna, where we studied the

foremost design in contemporary Europe under the tutelage of Joseph Binder, a close friend of Hans Hofmann. Binder kept emphasizing to us "Find the ground form," advice which was enlivened by his gesture with his thumb as though he were boring deeply into the sand.

After two weeks we went to Kitzbühel and studied—and marvelled at—the Tyrolean costumes, consisting of ornamented leather vests with white leather trousers fitting close to the men's legs, and red tassels on their mocassins and vests embroidered intricately with blue and green designs. The costumes were alike in general pattern but each one was different and unique. Then on to Hungary for two weeks, where the colors were deep purple and the vests and the aprons on the women were magenta, gay yellow and orange. We then went into Moravia in Czechoslovakia, the country through which the Moldau flows and which inspired Smetana's symphonic poem, "Bohemia's Fields and Forests." Here the colors were bright red-orange embroidered on billowing skirts, intermixed with pink and cerulean blue.

The peasant women told us that they had to wait in the autumn till their fingers lost their hard shell of skin from work in the fields and became tender enough for them to embroider their special costumes for weddings, which were stored in beautifully decorated treasure chests, and to paint designs on eggs, or flowers on the walls of their huts.

In each village the peasants were kind enough to put on a wedding ceremony for us, for which they dug deeply into their trunks to get out the costumes kept for special ceremonies. The head-dresses of the women made me think of the coronation of a queen, except that each queen here had her hair in a long braid down her back.

The folk dancing was entrancing though difficult for any of us trying to sketch the design on the dancer's stockings. But the peasant girls had no compunction about stopping and holding up their skirts so we could finish the sketch.

The music came from harmonicas and primitive one-string violins to keep time for the whirling figures in their bright colors. I shall never forget the experience of being whirled around by a peasant girl who did not come up to my shoulder but was, through long working in the fields and milking cows, as strong as the proverbial ox. It seems one can pick up the art of a village through one's bodily participation in its ceremonies.

The human species, especially in these more primitive villages, seems unable to repress the desire to adorn their clothes with every color of the spectrum, and to plant flowers so thick in front of their houses that you cannot walk between them. Sunflowers, hollyhocks, petunias and roses of all sorts—these and a conglomeration of other flowers filled what we would call the front yards. Then, as though this were not enough, the peasant houses were adorned on the outside by paintings in a band around the houses like abstract graffiti.

Thus began my devotion to art and to beauty. By the time I arrived back at the college in Saloniki in September, I was a quite different person.

*(drawing overleaf)*

Peasant's hut and yard in Czechoslovakia,
summer of 1932.

# CHAPTER II

# *Beauty* HAS
## KEPT ME *Alive*

*Beauty is indeed the sphere of unfettered*
*contemplation and reflection; beauty conducts us*
*into the world of ideas, without however*
*taking us from the world of sense. . . .*
*By beauty the sensuous man is brought back*
*to matter and restored to the world of sense.*

FRIEDRICH VON SCHILLER

## 2

HE TITLE of this chapter obviously does not refer to my physical life. That goes on automatically, as it does in billions of other people. I
write rather of a new quality of life which had begun
with the poppies and spread out to an awareness of the
colorful and adventurous aspect of life—the aspect of
beauty—which had been there all the time but which I
had never noticed. I seemed released from my old com-
pulsions: I felt empowered, freed for all kinds of activities. I brushed up on my French and found, to my
initial surprise, that there was a great deal of musical
and cultural life in Saloniki, that friends of different
nationalities were waiting, so to speak, for me to join
them.

Some of this change, I knew, was due to what I had

learned at Alfred Adler's seminar. But these experiences were then embodied in my life among the peasants with my fellow-painters. I could live out, imprint upon my psyche, the new ways of life learned psychologically; it crystallized my new understanding of beauty.

It seems fitting now, half a century later, to put down what I have learned and to note the later expressions of this mysterious and enriching fountain of life.

### What is Beauty?

Beauty is the experience that gives us a sense of joy and a sense of peace simultaneously. Other happenings give us joy and afterwards a peace, but in beauty these are the same experience. Beauty is serene and at the same time exhilarating; it increases one's sense of being alive. Beauty gives us not only a feeling of wonder; it imparts to us at the same moment a timelessness, a repose—which is why we speak of beauty as being eternal.

Beauty is the mystery which enchants us. Like all higher experiences of being human, beauty is dynamic; its sense of repose, paradoxically, is never dead, and if it seems to be dead, it is no longer beauty.

Most people in our culture suppress their reactions to beauty; it is too soul-baring. A session with a patient in therapy may illustrate our general cultural shyness in talking on this topic. I had been seeing this particular client, a woman, once a week for a year; always she talked about some practical problem, generally about the difficulties of getting along with her husband. Though I liked her and she was a highly intelligent person, her quarrels with her husband had become boring to me.

This hour she began by saying she was very weary,

they had had visitors for a week, she was "punch drunk," and didn't have much to say today.

So I suggested, since she was so fatigued, that she try free association, simply letting whatever popped into her mind come forth. I explained Freud's idea of free association: it's like looking out the window of a speeding train. Each view seems separated from the one before, but when you look down on the whole, as though from above, one can see it makes a meaningful landscape. She somewhat reluctantly agreed though she didn't believe it would do any good.

Following is a summary of the hour:

> The first thing that comes to me, I stopped my car on the way here to look at the twilight. It was just beautiful, the purple hues with the green hills behind them. . . . it is the most beautiful time of the day. . . . I don't believe in a God, at least in a personal God, there is so much evil in the world, it makes it so pointless. But when I see such beauty, I can't believe it is by accident. The poets in the country I come from speak of this time of day when they are writing the most important things—when they write of love and so on.

> In the twilight I used to go to the beach all alone, it was lovely . . . This time of day would be a good time to die, a good time to be alone. . . . I should have been a poet [smiling] . . . This time at twilight doesn't last long . . . It seems to say something about true love—it can't be actualized. [Silence]

> I would like to die at this time . . . It is so peaceful here in your office . . . I keep noticing the beauty outside the window . . . My mother called

from [another country] . . . called all the way to
tell me she has a cold . . . That ruins the beauty
. . . My mother always wanted me to notice the
beauty . . . to enjoy the world.

The bay is so beautiful . . . I stop each time I
drive toward the bridge . . . San Francisco seems
unreal, like a *fata morgana* . . . I am part of it
. . . it feels so good, I want to melt into it.

People come up to me, want me to take their picture with their camera, they stand right in front so
they block out all the picture [she laughs]. Maybe
I think other people ruin the scene.

When I was in the army [in another country], I'd
go swimming in the ocean at twilight, alone. It was
wonderful. Then the waves drove me out—they
seemed like monsters coming after me. The
mountains behind the ocean are great in twilight,
but they become monsters—big and dark—when
night falls.

At the end of the hour I asked her how she felt.
"Somewhat relaxed . . . like when I go to a good movie.
My friends want to talk about it, but not I . . . This
scene here [looking out my windows] is pure beauty."
She then expressed her fear that she had said nothing
today, maybe it was all superficial talk. I assured her
that no topics could be more important than beauty,
God, death. I added that I thought it was the most profound hour we had ever had.

This person is like the majority of people in our
western culture: we suppress our feelings of beauty; we
are shy about them, they are too personal. We talk about
"the view," anything to avoid the personal statement.
And if we do let out such feelings we apologize for them,

as this woman did in saying she was afraid it was all "superficial talk." It is fascinating how much beauty preoccupied this young woman, and yet she had never mentioned it before.

Each of us can give as examples of beauty only those experiences which have impressed us. Beauty is, to me, listening to Murray Perahia play a Mozart concerto. Beauty is standing under the grape arbor among lilacs in May when the air is heavy with their fragrance, faint for a moment and then filling the air suddenly again as though to intoxicate us.

My own experience of beauty has generally been of the simple things—a walk through pine forests beside the lake, snow in winter weighing down the limbs of spruce trees till they touch the ground. For me, beauty is watching the dawn when the limpid sky turns to pink and the pink to orange and then fiery red as the sun rises over the mountains like a god to change the whole face of the earth.

Early in the morning in summers in New Hampshire I walk out to my studio on the far edge of the meadow as the morning mist hangs in the air. The sun rises and its yellow rays rest on the mist. There is no human sound, only the song of thrushes in the bushes. On every blade of grass in the meadow there is a pearl-drop of dew, and as I pick a blade and look more closely I see on each pearl-drop its spectrum of color reflecting the sun, creating a meadow filled with trillions of tiny sparkling rainbows.

But in our culture, in our discursive language, we cannot talk too much of beauty. True, in poetry or in painting or in music we can communicate the experience. But beauty is a subjective vision at the same

moment as it is an objective datum, and we need to respect this wholeness, this union of experience. This is
why, when we are before an image of beauty, we in-
stinctively remain silent. We look and we listen. When
we talk too much about beauty, we are objectifying it,
putting it outside ourselves, destroying the inner vision
and reducing it to objective chatter. We must preserve
the capacity for wonder—which is the awareness that
we can never fully explain the inner experience of
beauty.

There is also a cultural reason why we do not talk
much about beauty. Our culture worships change. As
Don Michael puts it, we become bored instead of serene; and how then can we appreciate the sense of eternity, the timelessness of this experience? In our age "time
is money"; we construct great buildings only to tear them
down in seventy-five years. We erect the tallest edifice
in the world, the World Trade Center, an essentially
ugly pair of buildings which destroy the previously lace-
like loveliness of the skyline of New York, which was
one of the wonders of the world. Our age is not one in
which beauty has a firm place at the Board of Directors'
meeting.

We must nevertheless, being human, communicate
by words as much as we can.

On the desk where I write there is a plaster of Paris
cast of a life-size Greek head, sculpted, so I am told,
by Scopas about 390 B.C. Every time I went to Athens
while I was a teacher in Saloniki, I used to sit in contemplation before the original sculpture in the National
Museum. It is not too much to say that I fell in love
with the head of this goddess Hygeia. Decades later,
when I was in the Louvre I saw it among their casts,

and ran to the man in charge from whom I bought it for fifteen dollars.

An accurate copy of the original, the head is amazingly simple. The sense of repose, the calm expression, seem as eternal as the Milky Way. The strong nose coming down directly from the high forehead is authentically Hellenic; the mouth and eyes speak out of a history that knows no time. The slightly wavy hair is kept in place by a ribbon. We see in it the Greek ideal of beauty as both male and female. The masculine and feminine are merged, and only the hair gives the clue that this is a goddess and not a god.

But most important of all, there is no emotion shown in this face of Hygeia. It reveals the dignity of *being*, not feelings such as laughter or grief which come and go. It illustrates the secret of classic Greek beauty in that it comes from a level deeper than feelings; it is ontological. The greatness of Greek culture is that it does not tell us of emotions as such but speaks out of the center of being—Socrates would say the soul. This depth is in Greece's drama, in its philosophy and its temples, but most of all in these figures carved in marble. The sign of decadence, which was to come shortly after Scopas, is that sculptors, even Praxiteles, pictured emotions and not being.

For twenty-five centuries nothing has disturbed in the slightest the refined serenity of Hygeia's expression. My goddess looks out upon the world with the same emanation of eternity—a minute is an eon and an eon is a minute—which she has held ever since Scopas lifted his chisel and mallet to hammer out his vision in Pentelican marble. There come flooding into our minds the last lines of Keats' "Ode on a Grecian Urn,"

Cast of Hygeia by Scopas, 390 B.C.

When old age shall this generation waste,
    Thou shalt remain, in midst of other woe
Than ours, a friend to man, to whom thou say'st,
    Beauty is truth, truth beauty—that is all
        Ye know on earth, and all ye need to know.

*Beauty as Harmony*

Classical Greece was not afraid to talk of beauty. The Greeks had two ways of describing it. One was that beauty is the condition when everything fits, when in a scientific theory or the Parthenon one has the conviction that nothing could be added or subtracted. All the parts are in harmony with all the other parts. This was the definition which Aristotle liked; it fits the empirical enthusiasm which characterized him and his countless followers through the ages.

The other description of beauty, invented by Pythagoras and held by Plato and later by Plotinus, has nothing to do with parts. Beauty, rather, is the eternal splendor of the One showing through the Many. That is, in the many different forms in our universe, the One shines through and gives splendor and meaning to all. The former definition is more passive, the latter more active, as I shall indicate below.

When Plato considered the great trilogy of Beauty, Truth and Goodness, he placed Beauty at the top because Beauty is harmony, and whether Truth or Goodness are harmonious is the test of their integrity. Goodness gives a person self-respect, Truth gives gratification, but Beauty gives both peace and joy simultaneously. Plato believed that Goodness, or ethics, consists of acting in a way that is harmonious with your fellow human beings, and this makes the action testable by its beauty.

27

Indeed, the Greek word for beauty and for goodness is
the same, *"kalon."* When Rilke wrote his sonnet, "To
the Torso of the Unknown Apollo," and ended it with
the ethical challenge, "You must change your life," he
was accurately expressing the Greek view of life. And
when Socrates gave his enchanting prayer at the conclusion of the *Phaedrus,* "O Pan, and all ye other Gods that
haunt this place, give me beauty in the inward man,
and may the outward and inward man be at one," he
was illustrating again that ethics follows beauty.

The timelessness of beauty saves us from worship-
ping at the shrine of progress, or kneeling at the altar
to pray that tomorrow we will make more money than
today, and the future will be better than the past, until
we are caught up in a sordid merry-go-round that makes
it impossible for us to appreciate the delicious calm of
a moment of timelessness. The God who became Prov-
idence after the Renaissance, and then became Progress
after the Industrial Revolution, is not the God of beauty.
For beauty has nothing to do with progress. Who will
be so rash as to proclaim that our present buildings are
more beautiful than the Parthenon? Or our present
churches more beautiful than Chartres? Or our present
dishware more beautiful than the Greek vases? Or modern music better than Mozart and Bach? Beauty is beyond the confines of progress.

Progress must not be identified with evolution, a very
different thing. Even evolution does not guarantee that
our species and our world are getting better and better;
many species have been dropped out, and why should
we be evolution's darling? The one thing we can be
sure about is the timelessness of beauty. Let us, as Walter
Pater entreats us, seek the desire for beauty, the

experience of poetic passion, the love of art, the highest quality of each moment for its own sake.

That great explosion of creativity which occurred in Fifth Century Greece has bequeathed to us an endlessly rich mine of beauty in which to spend precious hours and days in the company of great spirits. The Greeks were willing to live and die for beauty, as I shall indicate in Chapter 9.

It is fascinating to note how the scientists have kept alive the sense of beauty since Grecian times. The astronomer Kepler believed his discoveries were in the direct line with Pythagoras, and that the revolution of the planets around the sun was beautiful in the same sense as the vibrations of a violin string are beautiful. No wonder he spoke of "the harmony of the spheres," and broke out in a cry of joy, "I thank thee, Lord God our Creator, that thou allowest me to see the beauty in thy work of creation." Kepler also wrote, "Mathematics is the archetype of the beauty of the world." I owe some of the above references to Werner Heisenberg, who himself held that beauty was central in his own discovery of the "Uncertainty Principle" in modern physics. Nobel Laureate in physics, Heisenberg pointed out that the researcher in physics recognizes truth by the splendor of its beauty.

We mistakenly assume that beauty is passive, which is no doubt the influence of our culture which does not have time to listen to the active powers of beauty. But listening is an active process. Ever since Plato, beauty has been experienced by sensitive persons as an active agent: it is the sign of the splendor of truth, and it speaks out through this splendor to the mathematicians, physicists, and all those who listen patiently. As Pythagoras said many centuries ago, "The stars in the heavens sing a music if we only had ears to hear." The apprehension of Platonic Ideas is an intuitive, half-conscious intimation, which sings to those who can hear. I would even propose that such splendor was speaking to me from the flock of poppies in the original field of flowers of which I made the sketch. What a lovely world we could live in if we would listen more frequently to this splendor!

Poincaré, the great contemporary mathematician, sounds like Plato when he asks the question of how new mathematical discoveries are made. Then he answers,

> The useful combinations are precisely the most beautiful, I mean those best able to charm this special sensibility that all mathematicians know. . . .

He goes on to speak of the mathematical theories that bubble up from the unconscious depths and adds that most of them do not affect the mathematician's aesthetic sensibility. "But only certain ones are harmonious, and, consequently, at once useful and beautiful." And these then turn out to be the valuable and eminent discoveries in the science of mathematics and physics.

### Schiller's Thoughts on Beauty

Many people, including myself, believe that the greatest and richest discourse on beauty in our Western culture was written by Friedrich von Schiller, just before 1800. Gifted dramatist that he was, and philosopher whose friendship Goethe treasured, Schiller gives a lengthy title to his discourse, "Letters Upon the Aes-

30

thetic Education of Man." Here we find amazingly penetrating insights into the meaning of beauty. Since most people have not read Schiller, we can best let him speak for himself.

"Beauty alone confers happiness on all, and under its influence every being forgets that he is limited." Schiller hastens to add that this forgetting is temporary, however, for the sense of limitations is crucial to our creating beauty. We actually create beauty out of the endeavor to come to terms with the paradox on one hand of freedom and on the other of destiny. Our limits come from being both nature and spirit, finite and infinite, objective and subjective. No one knows this struggle better than the artists, be they painters or musicians or sculptors or dancers or any other figures in the arts.

Artists wrestle with fate in the endeavor to make objective their inner subjective vision. Jim Lord, whose portrait was being painted by Alberto Giacometti, writes this about his artist,

> This fundamental contradiction, arising from the hopeless discrepancy between conception and realization, is at the root of all artistic creation, and it helps explain the anguish which seems to be an unavoidable component of that experience. Even as "happy" an artist as Renoir was not immune to it.
>
> What meant something, what alone existed with a life of its own was his [Giacometti's] indefatigable, interminable struggle via the act of painting to express in visual terms a perception of reality that had happened to coincide momentarily with my head [which Giacometti was then trying to paint]. To achieve this was of course impossible, because what is essentially abstract can never be made

concrete without altering its essence. But he was committed, he was, in fact *condemned* to the attempt, which at times seemed rather like the task of Sisyphus.

Out of such a struggle comes the superb Greek head which gazes serenely at me from the corner of my desk. The artists are doomed to failure, but out of their Sisyphean effort, they produce a sculpture or a painting or piece of music of genuine beauty, a gift to the world.

Being both finite and infinite—as Schiller describes this contradiction—our human imagination soars among the planets in the heavens but at the same time our feet are in the dust of the earth. *If there were no such limits in human life, there would be no beauty.* We hear of no great sculptor on Mount Olympus; Prometheus, the father of the human arts, is an outcast from Olympus.

Now the human being's radical disunity can temporarily achieve a unity by virtue of beauty. We hear the songs of the angels in the Angelus, we bow a moment to communicate with the infinite, yet we then return to digging potatoes with our hoes in the fields. Thus, no matter how much we object to our dual human nature, or how much we try to avoid it by taking on the cloak of religious or philosophical monism, we find ourselves still the plodding workers of the West. Enslaved as we are to our money-minded culture, we suppress our hunger for beauty and lose the chance to experience unity, as did my patient whose record was summarized earlier in this chapter.

The genuine if temporary release from this dilemma lies in beauty. It is the universal language which gives solace and serenity. It provides the sense of unity within ourselves which transcends, however temporarily, the grim paradoxes of life. Schiller says it is "only the unity of reality with the form, of the accidental with the necessary, of the passive state with freedom, that completes the conception of humanity." Again writes Schiller: "As soon as reason issues the mandate 'a humanity shall exist,' it proclaims at the same time the law, 'there shall be a beauty.' "

To those who try to flee from the realization of the dual nature of humankind, Schiller speaks sharply, "Nothing is more unwarrantable and contradictory than such a conception, because the aversion of matter and form, the passive and the active, feeling and thought is *eternal* and cannot be mediated in any way." He is saying that to be one-dimensional is the failure of life; we need to be aware that we are both determined and free.

Beauty is our way of meeting—not erasing—this dilemma. It brings its great boon precisely by virtue of its dealing with the nature of subjectivity and objectivity. For the "beautiful ought to temper while uniformly exciting the two natures, and it ought also to excite while uniformly moderating them." We try to avoid the paradox by being whole-heartedly the one or the other— the spiritual person who has the delusion that he has escaped from the senses, and the sensual person who has sacrificed his spirit. But Schiller would rebuke our sensuous culture, "Look to your form, to your spirit." I can imagine him saying, "be inspired by the richness of your thinking!" And to the spiritual man he would cry out, "Do not forget the richness of the world of the senses where all begins." For beauty is our second creator. "Nor is this inconsistent with the fact that she (beauty) only makes it possible for us to attain and

realize humanity. . . . For in this she acts in common
with our original creator, nature, which has imparted to
us nothing further than this capacity for humanity, but
leaves the use of it to our own determination of will."

Schiller's central idea—and inspiration, as I would call
it—is that beauty is born in play. When I first read this
I thought it a frivolous idea; but I then recalled that we
speak of Mozart and Beethoven *playing* the piano, the
very opposite of superficiality. And we refer to Shakespeare's *plays;* and I agreed that such "playing" describes the most profound and humanizing of all human
activities.

Play is the one activity where the fusion of inner vision and objective facts is achieved. Out of this comes
the *living form* which is beauty. This living form is vital,
alive, dynamic; and at the same time it gives serenity
and repose, as for example in music.

Play unites the inner world of our personal reverie
with the outer world of people and nature. "The object
of the play instinct, represented in a general statement,
may therefore bear the name of *living form*," asserts
Schiller, "a term that serves to describe all aesthetic
qualities of phenomena, and what people style, in the
widest sense, *beauty*." "A marble block, though it is and
remains lifeless, can nevertheless become a living form
by the architect and sculptor; a man, though he lives
and has a form is far from being a *living* form on that
account. . . . For this to be the case, it is necessary
that his form should be life, and that his life should be
a form. As long as we only think of his form, it is lifeless, a mere abstraction . . . . It is only when his form
lives in our feelings, and his life in our understanding,

that he is the living form, and this will everywhere be the case where we judge him to be beautiful."

This is why Otto Rank, one of the great pioneers in the early development of psychoanalysis, read Schiller and concluded that his idea of play is an accurate description of the psychologically healthy person. Rank believed that the goal of psychotherapy was to help the patient learn to create. The neurotic type of person, so Rank wrote in *Art and Artist,* was the *"artiste manqué,"* the artist who cannot create any art. All people are struggling to be creative in some way, and the artist is the one who has succeeded in this task of life. Thus creativity brings together what Freud summed up as the two purposes of life: to love and to work. Rank was only going further than Freud by pointing out that both of these, love and work, are aspects of creativity.

Now Schiller's idea, that beauty is the product of play, brings together the objective and subjective aspects of life. As Socrates put it in his prayer, the outward and inward man are at one. This is the description of the goal of psychotherapy. What we seek to do is to help each patient to become unified in him or herself, so that they can live out their lives with some integrity, some wholeness, some beauty.

This is what Schiller is talking about. Schiller gives not only a description of beauty, but a picture of the psychologically integrated human being. The neurotic is the one who cannot achieve this; healthy persons are the ones who can do it in their work and their love, whether they are painters or teachers or whatever they may be. The person who is integrated is thus the one who has learned to play in the sense which Schiller describes. Rank found in Schiller's essay a picture of the psychologically healthy person, one who overcomes the dilemma of life by *creating,* by *doing*—whether the doing involves sketching Greek poppies on a hillside or loving another human being.

That is what I meant, when I said at the beginning of this chapter, that beauty has kept me alive.

# CHAPTER III

## Visit TO THE Holy Mountain

*There is grandeur in this view of life, . . .*
*having been originally breathed by the Creator*
*into a few forms or into one; and that,*
*whilst this planet has gone cycling on*
*according to the fixed law of gravity,*
*from so simple a beginning endless forms most beautiful*
*and most wonderful have been and*
*are being evolved.*

CHARLES DARWIN

# 3

I T WAS cold on deck. An unexpected wind blew briskly across the bay from the Vardar Valley. We huddled together behind the boarding around the bridge walk in an effort to ward off the chilliness. Above us shone the bright stars, beyond the zig-zag line traced in the black sky by the tip of the foremast as it weaved back and forth; the gleaming stars charmed our eyes. The evening lights of Saloniki had been left far in the rear.

We found ourselves singing, as groups on shipboard

usually do—singing with the exuberance of elemental things, the racing wind, the swishing waves, the impenetrable inkiness of sea and heaven, and the dogged ploughing of the ship. On land the blow and the beat of the storm thrill one, but rarely do they scare, for *terra firma* seems always to be friendly. But at sea—as perhaps in the air—the daimonic elements are all around, above and below; one is a negligible item on the little speck called a ship, and the sheer indifferent power of the elements is terrifying.

My three companions, Hunter Mead, a teacher at Anatolia College, and two students, Olympios and Nicoledes, and I, were on our way to Mt. Athos, the Capital of the Monasteries of the Greek Orthodox Church. It was a week before Easter in 1932. This group of monasteries was a land unto itself, a thirty-mile-long peninsula separated from the mainland, a haven not only for the thousand monks and hermits on the peninsula but a land which no woman had visited since the eleventh century. It was, so I had heard, a land where silence and serenity were an essential part of its beauty. I sought neither the wisdom of men nor conversation with the monks. I wanted to be quiet with my own heart and open to my own spirit. I sought especially the answer to the question of the relationship of the beauty of nature to the Infinite, to what some people call the Absolute and others call God. It was thus a strange kind of expectancy that I felt as I sat with my companions on the ship's deck looking at the stars gleaming in the endless black void of nothingness.

Soon my three companions and I picked our way down the hazardous, steep, stepladder descent to our cabin. I rolled on to the hard bunk under the porthole, Mead turned in under me, and Olympios curled up on the other side. Poor Nicoledes piled his arms high with our spare coats and sweaters and bid us goodnight as he left to seek the least uncomfortable corner of the underdeck where third-class passengers must spend the night.

At three A.M. the steward awakened us. Daphne, our port on the peninsula of Athos, would be reached in one hour. Much will power was needed to tear ourselves from the warm embrace of sleep. Up on deck shortly, we looked across the calmed waters to see the black, pyramidal form of the Holy Mountain. A half moon peeked over it to play on the dark sea near our ship, and the stars scrutinized us in their sharp way, peering more brightly than the eyes of a cat at night.

Seated in the big rowboat they called a barque, which was waiting to push away from the well-illuminated steamer, we witnessed another act of the drama which proves everlastingly that man is not a particularly precious creature. The ship's captain was cuffing a little man in the barque, yelling ferociously in words which meant, we later learned, that the fellow had been a stowaway, and he must go back on ship to remain a prisoner till he could be turned over to the law in Saloniki. The poor man implored, but in vain—his cap was knocked into the black water from the Captain's blows—and finally, he was pushed up the gangway. Our barque moved out. Suddenly we heard a splash, then heavy puffing and the sound of swimming. Our oarsmen paused and the creature came near the edge of our little boat. True to the Greek character, an argument must take place as to whether or not he should be ac-

cepted into the barque and carried to shore or. . . .
The human heart won, and the little man, all dripping
and panting, fell onto a seat in front of us. We later
learned that he lived on a tiny island near Athos and
had no money to pay for passage on the ship.

We were mildly curious about what a land would be
like without women. No woman has set foot on Mt.
Athos since the eleventh century. One woman once
claimed that she had dressed like a man and visited the
holy land but the monks dispute this. Queen Marie of
Rumania proclaimed that she was planning to come to
Athos, but since you cannot refuse royalty, the monks
informed her that they would all kill themselves if she
did come; so she refrained.

A suggestion of gray in the sky brought us welcome
token that dawn would soon be upon us. Three or four
houses made up the village of Daphne. We stepped into
the coffee shop, weirdly lighted by gasoline lamps, and
waited the customarily long time for a Turkish coffee.
When we finally emerged into the open air, all around
us was the light purple of dawn. The one street of that
little town was dimly visible as it curved round the low
wooden buildings at the water's edge. Above the few
houses, the steep hills rose immediately. Then, with a
pleasant feeling beginning at one's nose and running
down to one's toes, we realized that it was spring. The
fragrance of the heavy blossoms of locust trees, the rich
perfume of wisteria, and the innumerable odors of the
hillside verdure, were to make our stay on the Holy
Mountain a visit to a natural paradise.

The office of the gendarme claimed our attention,
the officer, like practically everyone else on Athos, being

himself a monk in the usual long black gown and in-
verted-stove-pipe hat. One must get visas to enter this
special little kingdom, a peninsula thirty miles long and
about five miles wide. With us as we answered the
questions of the gendarme and surrendered our pass-
ports, was a silent priest whose figure and face arrested
our attention. He was tall and stood with natural dignity
and grace of figure; his face was delicate, sensitive, intelligent. His clear blue eyes especially attracted us. We
had seen him in the coffee shop, where he had quietly
waited for coffee, which should have shown us that he
was not native to this part of the globe. We had talked
about him, finding him unusual for an inmate of Athos.
The need to translate some of the gendarme's words
brought him into conversation with us. He had a pleas-
ing English accent and a rich, expressive voice; he told
us he was going to several of the monasteries to meditate and to study the rich treasures of Byzantine art and
hagiography possessed by Mt. Athos. We later learned
that he was a Benedictine monk of high British family.

The first lap of our journey had to be made on foot.
In high spirits in the early morning light, we pushed
along the half-path, half-road that led up the hillside.
We tossed several parting glances back over the roofs of
Daphne, which was now clearly visible in the early
morning. The birds had risen with the lavender dawn;
from the bushes on either side came the exhilarating
trills of warblers, the merry chirps of sparrows and a
not-too-well-blended chorus of notes from countless other
feathery creatures.

The stone road led up through a valley where the
blossoming lemon and orange trees of this Easter season

were exuberant with their delicate bright shades. They unceasingly tempted us to pause, like the mythological Circe, with their intoxicating odor—but our muscles were responding like tuned violin strings and we had no choice but to continue up the beckoning path.

After a happy hour's walk, we crossed a bridge and reached our first monastery. It was called Xerepatamou, from which one can translate that the tumbling stream was really the river of Xerxes. The thirty-mile-long peninsula had not escaped the Persian hordes who came over from Asia Minor to destroy Greece in 490 and 480 B.C. and were turned back at Marathon and Salamis. Xerxes had dug a canal so that his ships could cut across the peninsula without going around the great mountain rising there on our right.

Stepping into the stone court, we were met by one of those black-gowned, slowly moving figures, illustrated on the following page, who were to be our hosts and companions for the week. He spoke to us in a low, quiet voice, shook hands not very enthusiastically but with a bit of a smile of welcome on his lips. Under his black hat, graying hair hung more or less neatly, and his gray eyes caged something like a twinkle together with a look of intelligence. He took us up the dark wooden stairs and through the hall of the monastery to the guest room. Here we waited for our refreshments—after foregoing a look into the dining room that our host wished to show us, for the several servant monks he called out could not, in spite of much fumbling through the dusty corners, find the key. From the windows of the guest room we were thrilled by a view of the sea way below, nestling its pale blue translucency close to the foot of the bushy hills.

Greek monk
Rollo May, April '32

We were to become very accustomed to the refreshments the paddle-footed, dusty-gowned servant brought us: a bowl of orange preserves, from which we took a spoonful, a glass of water, into which we dropped our spoons and from which we quenched our thirst, a wee cup of Turkish coffee, and above all, a little glass of "ouzo," that fire water of the Greeks. Strong drink consummated! My companion Olympios refused, Nicoledes downed his with a gulp, Mead sipped half of it, and I found that merely to taste mine sufficed to send a surge of warmth through my whole body.

Three shaggy-haired horses were dragged out to carry us to our second destination, Karyes, the capital of the little Holy Kingdom. The Greeks more accurately term these creatures "*zoa*" (meaning "animals"), since the worn-out, eternally tired beasts more resembled mongrels bred of all known four-footed creatures than real horses. Riding on wooden saddles is not at all the last word in comfort, especially when the saddles are made extremely wide and the beast underneath moves with a succession of little stumbles. But we learned to ride side-saddle, much easier on one's skeleton.

When you go to Karyes you plod along the stone road up through a thickening pine forest. The trees about us were charming; my starved eyes, unfed on sights of real woods for many months in alien, barren, mid-eastern lands, feasted with supreme delight on green leaves and branches of pine needles and tall trunks of sycamores. Every whiff of the pungent perfume of pines set me to quivering with pleasure. The pine boughs on the narrow path brushed our cheeks and tickled our necks from time to time, as though the trees had been given a magic

Drawing of the monastery
of Simonopetra

power of recognizing us in this holy land. If I seem inclined toward overstatement, it is because the natural delights of those hills of Athos were so keen that one feels anything but his widest brush and most brilliant paint is inadequate.

Seesawing back and forth on the saddles as our horses plodded up the twisting road, we gave ourselves over to indolent enjoyment of the scenes around us. Here stretched a clearing, a wide green lawn among the pines, in the center of which a lone house kept guard. No doubt it was a "skete," a house where several hermits lived in perpetual silence. There, higher up in the forest, wood choppers flashed axes leisurely, bringing to our ears a half second later the thud of axe in wood. Pine poles and lumber, we were later to discover by the shiploads of it being handled at the coastal monasteries and the occasional donkey trains hauling it down the mountainsides, are among the few exports of the Holy Mountain. On the following page is a sketch I made of the "skete."

Finally our little caravan reached the top of the backbone of the peninsula. To our right rose the cold, hard, black-streaked-with-white snow outlining the sides of Mt. Athos itself. The blotches of snow near its sharp peak caught our eye, as, indeed, did the sheer beauty itself of the jagged but symmetrical outline of the mountain. Way at the top, over 6,000 feet above the sea, there hid among puffs of cloud a microscopic chapel.

Turning then to the left, we continued our way down the well-wooded hillside to Karyes, a large nest of monastic medieval stone buildings and churches with many

A "skete" at Mt. Athos
drawn April 27, 1932

round domes, some of which climb up into needle-like spires which we assumed were Russian Orthodox.

Practically all the inhabitants of that village-capital of the Holy Mountain were monks, sombre creatures who moved noiselessly along the curving stone streets with their black gowns flowing. We were struck by the feminine-like faces and bearing of many of the younger inhabitants—boys hardly twenty. That might mean, we opined, that living in a country without women tends to make men more feminine. When we watched a monk walking down the street with his gown flowing, we would have sworn it was a woman. A man becomes a double sex, no doubt, when there are no women with whom to polarize his maculinity. Or it might be due, on the other hand, to a desire on the part of the older monks for the company of young men who resembled the androgynous statues in the Athens Museum. I recalled the Greek ideal of figures who are both male and female shown in its statues, as we saw so beautifully in Hygeia.

Our letters of recommendation were accepted and permission to visit the different monasteries was given us by the "High Council," the ruling body of monks. This group consisted of a delegate from each monastery, large dignified men whom to look at was to respect. One with a massive, well-formed face in the midst of an abundant growth of colorful red hair, was a fellow I could well imagine in the Patriarch's chair at Constantinople. Several years of meditation at Athos seemed to be prerequisite for election to this high ecclesiastical chair in Eastern Orthodoxy.

The High Council put its seal together. There were five parts, each in the custody of a different branch of the government, and these parts were handed over and screwed together, the whole seal thus symbolizing the consent of all. Then they stamped our letter of entrance to the monasteries, accepted our fee of 100 drachmas, and bid us a formal and courteous adieu.

We knew that hermits had settled in caves in these cliffs before the little country of Mt. Athos itself was founded in the tenth century. Ever since, it had been the Holy Mountain for Greek and Russian and other Eastern Orthodox churches. When the Turks conquered Greece in the fifteenth century, the Sultan had exacted such a severe annual tribute from the monks that the monasteries had been impoverished. Then came in the early 1800s the Greek War of Independence, that war in which Byron had died fighting for the Greeks, after writing some of his most gripping heroic poems. I recall some of these by heart:

> The mountains look on Marathon
> And Marathon looks on the sea;
> And musing there an hour alone,
> I dreamt that Greece might still be free.
> And standing on the Persians' grave
> I could not deem myself a slave.

The Turks had again pillaged the priceless libraries of Athos, seizing the Romanesque bronze and gold ornaments. Even so, the monasteries still possessed the greatest collection of Byzantine and medieval manuscripts in existence. Finally the monasteries were put under the jurisdiction of the Patriarch in Constantinople.

The village of Karyes was like a city of the dead.

Silent as a cemetery at midnight, the only moving things in the village were the black-shrouded inmates. Through dirty store windows could be seen canned fish, eggs, and dusty packages, but there was practically no buying and selling. Most of the monks looked at us strangely, as though people from a planet they did not know had dropped into their streets, and their slightly-staring but otherwise expressionless faces registered very little welcome for us.

In the afternoon we made the half hour's walk to another monastery, Koutloumousiou, where we planned to spend the first night. It was, unfortunately, one of the poorer settlements, and so our first impression of monastic life was not entirely favorable. From the wide inner court, on all sides of which rose up storeys of windows and porches of the rooms of the monks, the unenthusiastic host led us up old wooden stairs to a wide parlor, where we were to sleep on the window seats.

One saving feature of this depressing place, however, was the view from the porch braced out high over a cliff at one end of the dark hall. Across a valley of olive trees and spring wheat, and over a forest of pines, Mt. Athos majestically filled the sky.

On this porch we sat as the sun went down with queer color-effects of pink and cream and orange as its rays pierced the clouds over the sea. We chatted with several of the monks: one young chap, twenty-five perhaps, newly arrived from Piraeus, carried a harrassed look on his face. That fellow, we thought, had found life too difficult as a shoemaker in Piraeus and had come to sample monastic life. But it apparently was not for him, and his worried, ill-at-ease expression foretold that

Koutmoulousiou, 1933

he would leave ere his period of three years' probation was up.

At sundown we stepped into the church for a few moments. As in all Greek Orthodox churches, the odor of incense was heavy. In the gloom we could make out the ikons and pictures on silver relief and the limitless conglomeration of brass chandeliers and other trappings. In the corner, somewhat better lighted by a little Romanesque window, a monk leaned against one of the high chairs around the inside wall of the church, arguing theology with a Greek who had just returned from America and was considering entering the order. The monk seemed to think he knew all about theology; and the would-be one, a man of rather simple mind, discussed with all the fervor of an active mouth, a swinging arm and an ill-informed brain.

Living in the open air most of the time (though the monasteries themselves were often stuffy enough), we slept heartily at night with no effort at all. But the beds! Totally springless, with boards under the thin mattresses, one might as well have been on the floor. The beds had been inhabited by others until the blankets smelled like a stable—and every night but one, I think, those friendly little fellows of the black and red insect species fed on our bodies. But it is amazing how little difference these things make when one has gotten into the monastic mood and accepts nature as the monks do.

The next morning was a happy time as we jogged on our horses up little hills and down into valleys, around and back over an ever-interesting stone path. The stumbling horses' hoofs crushed massive groups of blossoms on the path's edge. So abundantly did the flowers grow that there was no spot without spring blossoms waving in the breeze—brown-eyed susans, daisies, petunias, Indian paint-brushes and many flowers we did not know.

Over occasional green fields, we could see the tops of various "sketes," and the picturesque domes of St. Andrew, the school of the Russian monks. Farther on, lying softly against the curving shoreline, was the noon-quiet sea. And even more distant we could make out the bleak shape, dimmed by morning mist, of the island of Thasos. This was followed in the distance by the hardly perceptible lines of the island of Samothrace, from which came the Winged Victory now standing in the Louvre. This statue had once ornamented a Greek ship, before the ship sank in the sea near Samothrace.

Turning suddenly as the road bent, we saw far below, where a fertile, wooded valley sloped down to meet the sea in a wide, semi-circular white beach, the many-colored roofs of a little city seemingly plucked from the *Arabian Nights*. This monastery, Vatopedi, richest of the group, seemed magically placed there among the pines. Even more picturesque did it appear when we approached its walled exterior.

A genial cook, who had almost achieved the status of a monk though he wore no black gown, gave us a cordial welcome to Vatopedi. We sucked down the several spoonfuls of preserves, plunged the spoon into the glass of water, sipped the coffee and the ouzo, and felt so amazingly invigorated that we walked down into the broad courtyard immediately to explore our edifice from *Arabian Nights*. We went through the flour mill and blacksmith shop and other buildings which made this monastery a little city all by itself.

When we returned to our rooms, we found they looked

over the medieval courtyard. Hunter Mead—who was something of a medievalist—was delighted by the stone pavement, the brick refectory and red church in the center, the bell tower and clock tower (this last with the customary iron man posted on high to lift his hammer-hand and strike the hours). The porches and arcades of the monks' rooms completely surrounded the courtyard. All of this was truly medieval and almost too pictur-esque to be true. At Vatopedi, contradictory though it felt, modernism had crept in so far that the monks had electric lights and kept chickens!

The cook was also table waiter (though two andro-gynous creatures, presumably males, shuffled their un-kempt forms around the kitchen and then hovered over our table, as if they were waiters). The cook apologized for the bill of fare. He hoped we realized that since this meal was in *"megalē evthamada,"* which means the week before Easter, all the monks were fasting, and bean soup and bread were the only staples procurable. Oh, a week on bean soup and that hard, dark, packed-sawdust bread with its slightly sour taste! Before that week was over any one of our party would have committed murder had the word "beefsteak" been uttered.

The natural surroundings of Vatopedi were especially beautiful even for Athos. Just beyond the great gate in the wall you come to a turnstile letting you on to a pretty little footpath which twists enticingly up the valley. As you follow this path you tread on wide, flat stones. On your left is a little stone aqueduct in which the stream of clear water hurries past, bobbing with shadows and light from the sun filtering through the leaves of the omnipresent trees. On your right you peer down through the abundant foliage into a deep valley, the echoing

56

sound of tumbling water telling you that another brook below cuts its deep course toward the sea. For hours you amble around the curves of this enchanting pathway, leading higher up the valley, and always around you are the bright pink of Judas trees in full blossom, and the rich odors of lilies, and the scent of orange blossoms.

Wandering around the courtyard during the twilight interim before supper, we happened into the monastery ovens, the tiny building in which the bread is baked. A huge-bodied monk, nicknamed Friar Tuck by Mead, stretched his black-bearded face into a broad grin to welcome us. The first thing about him that impressed us was his great, heavy face, in which black eyes twinkled under shaggy hair; and the second was the dirtiness of the several heavy, blanket-like black robes wrapped around his body and secured with a rope at his waist. A man with probably very little brain compared with his powerful brawn, he appeared almost happy that his wife and child had died and he had been free to leave the troublesome life of the city for monastic serenity, about which he was certainly enthusiastic. Later we met him coming out of church, his eyes aglow with wonder and awe and worship, as though he had seen Christ himself literally rising from the tomb.

In another part of the monks' quarters (Vatopedi being "idiorythmic," the monks enjoyed individual rooms where they prepared their own meals) we met an old fellow with a face like that of Leonardo da Vinci. He hobbled into his room behind us, and told us that he had lived a great part of his ninety years in that monastery. Two student initiates made up another part of the interesting company with which we talked at

Vatopedi; one was blue-eyed, soft-voiced, and slightly feminine with his long hair. The other was a typical college chap with a large, well-formed face, genial black eyes, and an almost hail-fellow-well-met manner. He would have been more in place on the tennis team or at the Varsity Prom than at Athos. Indeed, we observed him later at church where he seemed restless and not absorbed in things monastic. Perhaps he was one of those young men of ability who go through Athonian training as a stepping stone to high ecclesiastical position in the Greek Orthodox Church.

After a rough meal—saved by the fact that the cook with great pride brought on the luxury of "halvah," a rich Greek confection made of honey and almonds—we were invited into the parlor to meet the monastery doctor. He was a braggart who carried his wide travels and vast experience very much on his sleeve. He sat in his white robe at a table in the center of the room, and insisted on being the center of all conversation—for which he was well-fitted since he shifted with no difficulty from Greek to English to French to Turkish, ad infinitum. Boasting of his unbelief, he was in sentiment certainly no monk. He said he was a monastery doctor only for the salary.

At several monasteries we were shown part of the vast manuscript treasury of Athos—the richest in early manuscripts of the Greek Church. They were ponderous books full of charming color-work and design. In the life-like paintings of birds, we observed, true to the word of Professor Papadopoulos who had explained the matter to us at Pantocratos, there were traces of classic art persisting through Byzantine times.

At one parlor-session we became better acquainted

with the Serbian, a newspaperman we had met on the boat and with whom we crossed routes several times while at the Holy Mountain. A friendly fellow with a wee, turned-up nose and Slavic table manners which were totally without refinement, we liked him, and we were amused to discover later on that he was an outstanding Dalmatian poet. It began to dawn on me that an amazingly large number of writers had come to Athos searching for something. What was it—some refreshment of the soul? After all, it was why I was there as well.

We left Athos at the conclusion of our week by the same ship that brought us there, except that it now sailed at noon instead of in the dark of night. As we steamed out of the harbor I leaned on the railing, looking back at the cerulean sea comforting the shore of Mt. Athos. I knew I would never forget the old monk who looked like Leonardo da Vinci, or Friar Tuck, or the cook who was so proud of his halvah.

That noon as I stood by the ship's rail I was thinking especially of the Easter service at the monastery of Stavronikita. The little Byzantine church in the center of the compound had been filled with smoke from the hundreds of candles flickering from every conceivable perch in the walls. Some faint light filtered through the slits in the wall of the church giving a mystical aura to the icons hanging from the ceiling. The service had gone on all night long when we came to it early in the morning. For once the monks had seemed all-believing.

At the conclusion of the service we filed in front of the abbot, who, while giving each of us three Easter eggs wrapped in a veil, greeted us with the words, *"Christos Anesti!"*—which means "Christ has risen." To which each of us responded, according to the custom, *"Alēthos Anesti!"*—"Truly He has risen." I remember that I had been seized then by a moment of spiritual reality: what would it mean for our world if He had truly risen? Oh, I had known all the criticisms of the monastic life on Mt. Athos, how easily it could be lampooned by the skeptics and the activists. How easily one could joke about the inconsistency of excluding women when the little land itself is dedicated to the Virgin Mary. But what was the particular spiritual quality of this place, what was its genie?

It came from the beauty of the mountain and foothills, which seemed as though nature had portioned out her secrets guardedly elsewhere but here had lavished every kind of beauty from its treasure chest. I was aware that I had not come to see and talk with persons, neither the monks nor my friendly companions, and this is why I have mainly left them out of my account. I had been almost entirely preoccupied with nature and what its beauty could mean. For there I had felt a door open, and I could glimpse a kind of religion very different from the often rigid faith of the monks. Like Wordsworth's, my experience was, and is, of

> A presence that disturbs me with the joy
> Of elevated thoughts; a sense sublime
> Of something far more deeply interfused,
> Whose dwelling is the light of setting suns,
> And the round ocean and the living air,
> And the blue sky. . . .

The ship began to turn north into the Aegean Sea, and I took my last look at the Holy Mountain, alternately white and pure as the snow covering its peak, and black as the secretive daimonic in the inner life of each one of these monks and each one of us human beings.

As I reflect, I call to mind the sensitive persons, especially writers, who have gone to Athos as modern-day pilgrims to awaken their hearts, to find answers to fundamental questions, to re-kindle some inner spiritual reality. A surprising number of authors have gone there to restore their souls in the silence and the serenity to be found at Athos. The modern Greek novelist, Nikos Kazantzakis, when a young man, had come there with a companion some twenty years after we were here. He had been seething with spiritual confusion.

"I did not know what I was going to do with my life," so writes Kazantzakis. "Before anything else I wanted to find an answer, my answer, to the timeless questions. . . ."

In the course of his walks, Kazantzakis had long talks with monks like our Leonardo and with hermits in caves on the cliffs over the Aegean Sea.

He tells how he confessed to one Holy Man his inner struggles. The Ascetic answered, "Woe is you, woe is you, unfortunate boy. You shall be devoured by the mind; you shall be devoured by the ego— the 'me,' the self."

Kazantzakis took his leave with the statement, "Tell God it is not our fault but His—because he made the world so beautiful."

As Kazantzakis and his companion left Athos, he pointed to an almond tree in bloom, and cried, "Angelos, during the whole of this pilgrimage our hearts have

61

been tormented by many intricate questions. Now, behold the answer!"

And his friend, in answer, recited the little poem,

> I said to the almond tree,
> Sister, speak to me of God.
> And the almond tree blossomed.

It dawned upon me as I re-read these words from Kazantzakis that this is what had gripped me so deeply at Athos—the almond tree that worships God by blossoming and the tenderness of those lemon blossoms in the springtime. And this is why I include the account of our trip in this book. How delicate, how fragile, was the whole land every spring. Yet the whole thirty-mile little country would be obliterated by one modern bomb. There was such a stark contrast there among medievalism, natural beauty and modernity, that every visitor's life is brought up against the stark reality of beauty's closeness to death.

And is beauty an answer, a way of making that choice to live and create without cringing, without hiding one's self from the daimonic? For beauty, as Schiller and countless others of our sensitive forebears have proclaimed, confronts and absorbs the daimonic into the whole, absorbs the shadow into the light, brings holiness into what would otherwise be a meaningless, destructive void.

I am certain that it was the beauty of nature along the pathways which led from monastery to monastery which gave me my own glimpse into eternity, and this came side by side with the medieval worship of a medieval god. I felt some replenishment, some re-kindling of my own spirit. Coming only a month after my own pilgrimage up Mt. Hortiati and the experience with the poppies I have described in the first chapter, I had been surely impressionable and spiritually hungry. I was indeed ready for the experience of Athos. The serenity of those moments was worth my preserving forever. Wordsworth wrote directly after the lines quoted above,

> Therefore am I still
> A lover of the meadows and the woods
> And mountains. . . .

And I too am still a lover of the orange blossoms and the pine groves and the bubbling streams. I knew that the flowers and the spring verdure were not in themselves God. But are we not given a glimpse of the beauty of God by these gay trumpetings of brilliant pink of the flowering Judas trees, and by the lemon blossoms with their magical odor and by the heavily scented lavender of the wisteria hanging from every branch?

Beauty is not God, but it is the resplendent gown of God and of our spiritual life. Such a thought grasped Keats, who wrote:

> Beauty is truth, truth beauty—that is all
> Ye know on earth, and all ye need to know.

Yes. But there were still things I yearned to know. Is beauty at least our pathway to the spirit? Is beauty the gateway to spiritual enchantment and to the serenity of eternity? Is beauty related to the eternity of death? The quest described in this book is an endeavor to answer some of these questions.

# PART · II

# CHAPTER IV

# *Beauty*
## AND *Death*

*Death is the mother of beauty.*

WALLACE STEVENS

*4*

HEN PEOPLE are on the verge of death they
think, strangely enough, about beauty. Many of
these thoughts are about how beautiful is this
earth that they are about to leave.

A friend in his forties was dying of cancer. He spent
his last days on the sun-porch in a deck chair thinking,
as he expressed it, "How beautiful each day is!" The
psychologist Abraham Maslow, who lived on the Charles
River west of Cambridge, had had a severe heart attack
and feared another. During this period he was describing his change in attitudes in a letter in which he said,
"My river has never seemed so beautiful."

We find the same thing in great drama. Just before
the ending of Ibsen's "Peer Gynt," when Peer is pondering his misspent life and anticipating his death, he

speaks of beauty in some of the most beautiful lines of
the play:

> How unspeakably poor a soul can be
> When it enters the mist and returns to nothing!
> O beautiful earth, don't be angry with me
> That I trod your sweet grass to no avail.
>
> O beautiful sun, you have squandered
> Your golden light upon an empty hut.
> There was no one within to warm and comfort.
> The owner, I know now, was never at home. . . .
>
> Then let the snow pile over me,
> And let them write above: "Here lives no one."
> And afterwards—let the world take its course.

But I do not believe that leaving the earth explains
fully this relation of beauty to death. More important in
such crisis situations is that aspect of beauty that transcends death. Beauty calls up in us the qualities that go
beyond death, such as eternity, serenity, the use of the
imagination to project us beyond time and space, even
to Peer Gynt's imagining the snow piling over him after
he dies.

This is what Schiller meant when he related beauty
to the human paradox of life and death. Only when we
confront death, in some form or other, only when we
realize that life is fragile, do we create beauty. It is parallel to the fact that only when we confront death do
we authentically love.

The line "Death is the mother of beauty," quoted at
the head of this chapter, comes from Wallace Stevens's
poem "Sunday Morning." The line actually appears twice

in that poem, and in one of these instances Stevens wrote:

> Death is the mother of beauty; hence from her
> Alone shall come fulfillment to our dreams
> And our desires.

Some thoughts may help us toward an answer to the questions this troubling line raises.

Nature, for example, shows how obviously true Stevens's "Death is the mother of beauty" is. The incredibly wonderful colors of autumn leaves, say in Vermont, are a species of death. The leaves are most beautiful as they die, and because they die. We also know that the immortal gods on Mt. Olympus who had no death were thoroughly bored with their lives. The life on Olympus consisted mostly of pranks and tricks to liven up their lethargic existence; there was no creation of any significance that went on among the gods as such. But when Zeus or some other god got interested in a mortal woman, then something creative did happen. Only when death was introduced into the boring drowsiness of Olympus did the home of the gods get stirred up and alive. It is a very puzzling thought _that without death, there would be no beauty_.

Death is the mother of beauty also in the sense that death is a setting of ultimate limits. We all know we will die, and we already receive a forewarning of these limits in illness and great fatigue. But death is the final and perpetual boundary. Limits are an aspect of form, and are thus one aspect of beauty. We are all _condamnes_, as Victor Hugo says, "We are all under sentence of death but with a sort of indefinite reprieve." The artists know this most clearly, and hence are the ones who create things which last beyond death.

The artists partake of eternity in that they, after death, are offering something to future generations. The artists seek to overcome the boundaries of life, to gain a kind of eternity in their creative work amid the ephemeral days we humans pass together. The artist leaves a gift for us and for the future. No one can look at the ceiling of the Sistine chapel without realizing that the irascible Michelangelo has left his spirit, in a series of forms, that give a sense of eternity to those of us who live four centuries later, and I think this effect will last as long as humankind inhabits this planet.

Beauty is eternity born into human existence. A chord of music, such as the one that opens Beethoven's "Hammerklavier Sonata," sets loose within us a quality of eternity, a sense that this moment is ultimate. One thinks, "I could live or die tomorrow but *now I have this moment.*" It is a quality of life, not a place nor a new life, that gives our present life this experience of eternity.

Spinoza adjures us, as we recall from his *Ethics*, to live *"sub specie aeternitatis,"* that is, "under the light of eternity." He then goes on to say that eternity is existence itself, for "the existence of a thing cannot be explained by duration or time, but only by this quality of eternity." When the setting sun sends amber rays through the mystic blues of the high clerestory windows in the Cathedral of Chartres, I find myself breathing a kind of silent prayer, "May this moment last forever!" It is like the lines of Faust,

> Then to the moment I could say:
> Linger you now, you are so fair!

Foreknowledge comes, and fills me with such bliss,
I take my joy, my highest moment this.

The fact is that the clock does go on, our duration does plague us, and death comes closer every moment. But it is irrelevant if we heed Spinoza's words and carry with us *aeternitas,* the capacity to live under the light of eternity, which is the light of beauty.

For this is what beauty does for us, in the grace that beauty brings us, in death as the mother of beauty. All of these are but ripples of life on the sea of eternity.

In any discussion of the curious relationship between beauty and death, we need to consider the war poetry, the poems written by young men amid the utter cruelty and ugliness of warfare, where at any moment one may be struck dead. There is Rupert Brooke,

If I should die, think only this of me;
    That there's some corner of a foreign field
        That is forever England. . . .

And think, this heart, all evil shed away,
    A pulse in the eternal mind, no less
        Gives somewhere back the thoughts
    By England given;

Her sights and sounds; dreams happy as her day;
    And laughter, learnt of friends; and gentleness,
        In hearts at peace, under an English heaven.

And Alan Seeger,

I have a rendezvous with Death
    At some disputed barricade
        When Spring comes round with rustling shade
And apple blossoms fill the air. . . .

God knows 'twere better to be deep
  Pillowed in silk and scented down,
Where love throbs out in blissful sleep,
  Pulse nigh to pulse, and breath to breath,
Where hushed awakenings are dear. . . .
  But I've a rendezvous with Death
  At midnight in some flaming town,
When Spring trips north again this year,
  And I to my pledged word am true,
  I shall not fail that rendezvous.

Or John McCrae,

  In Flanders fields the poppies blow
  Between the crosses, row on row, . . . .

  We are the Dead. Short days ago
  We lived, felt dawn, saw sunset glow,
  Loved and were loved, and now we lie
    In Flanders fields.

Countless other young men are inspired in this confrontation with death to turn the experience into beauty. These citations are from World War I, but the same can be said about World War II. It is a phenomenon to be pondered: what is there in the threat of death in muddy trenches and in the grime and the fatigue of war, waiting for possible death in battle tomorrow, that should lead these men to turn their thoughts to the beauty of poetry?

As they go through the routine of life in the trenches these young men put words together to make poetry to console first of all their own hearts, and then to communicate with a wider, unknown world that will follow them. The verses sublimate the ugliness of the trenches and blot out the stench of their present life by remembering the odor of "apple blossoms filling the air." Their deep loneliness is covered over by the memories of times when they "loved and were loved."

We could apply here all the usual psychological clichés with some accuracy: the poems are a "compensation" for the ugliness of their surroundings, they are a "reaction formation" to the anxiety of the proximity of death; the noble thoughts counteract the evil in which they are forced by custom and self-respect to participate. But though these interpretations are correct as far as they go, it seems a sacrilege to believe that they cover the profound question of the relation of beauty to death.

We owe it to these young poets to emphasize that in the poetry they achieve, and pass on to us, there is a serenity despite, or even because of, the conflict of which they are a part. It is not surprising, as one thinks about it, that in the ugliness of the trenches they yearn for the timelessness of beauty, and they long for the sense of repose that comes in beauty. The experience of inner harmony they pass on to us, seeking inner peace where there is no outer peace, as a guide to those who live after them. Nor is it surprising that they ponder whatever harmony of the spheres they can create in their imaginations, and cherish it to their heart. We transcend our fate, as these soldiers do, by the beauty of poetry.

These soldiers are thus able to confront the fear and anxiety that is endemic in wartime. In this respect the beauty of poetry enables them to achieve the aim of all good therapy, namely to help the person to raise repressed conflicts into consciousness, and to confront the fact that their danger only condenses into a short time what all of us have to face over the longer period of life itself. Their works bring into consciousness their underlying fears and anxieties, and do it in the highest form of consciousness, namely beauty.

These young poets, like other sensitive people, long to make of their senseless deaths a genuine tragedy which, on a deeper level than the futility of warfare, it actually is. As in the tragedy of O'Neill's "The Iceman Cometh," there is a deeper *sense of nobility which is present by the very vividness of its absence on the stage.* In this sense the useless death of any youth is a tragedy, and this tragedy makes perhaps our clearest picture of beauty. In this question we may find some explanation of why humankind goes to war century after century. Though we always rationalize our participation in the wars of our country, we know as we look backward over human history that the need to fight wars is an expression of the great and fundamental tragedies of our human fate.

My hunches about the intimate relation between beauty and death have, over the course of my life, led to the understanding that just as psychological "breakdown" and pathology can become important sources of artistic creativity, so the impulse to wage wars in which our youngest and best lose their lives seems somehow linked to that same irresistible attraction of (to quote Walt Whitman) "lovely and soothing death."

Though I write today as a psychologist with many decades of clinical experience behind me, some of my earliest inklings of the "beautifully tragic" take me back once more to Greece, to a young man named Costas, an elevator-operator in an Athens hotel. It was Costas who first led me to confront my deepest feelings about the complex linkage between death and beauty, tragedy and war. Though Costas is a character built up from a number of actual Greek boys I have known, boys who went through almost exactly his own experiences, he represents the complex linkage between death and beauty, tragedy and war. His story is told in the chapter which follows.

# CHAPTER V

## *We* ARE OF *Argyros*

*But no good supplants a good,*
*Nor beauty undoes beauty. Sophocles*
*Will carve and carry a fresh cup, brimful*
*Of beauty and good, firm to the altar foot. . . .*

ROBERT BROWNING

# 5

FIRST MET Costas in a hotel in Athens. To say I met him is not quite accurate—I was first attracted by his laugh as he stood near his elevator. I turned to observe him, but my eyes were still blinded by the dazzling light from the street.

I had just crossed Constitution Plaza in the heart of Athens, and the midmorning sun, reflected from the concrete pavements beneath my feet and the ivory-colored Pentelicus marble of the buildings on all sides of the Plaza, had rendered my eyes almost useless. There is no spot in the world quite so bright as Athens on a July morning. The tens of thousands of little whitish houses, some pink or yellow-tinted, toss the sunlight back and forth like mirrors.

Even the mountains lying low around the city like a great horseshoe add their glowing yellow-brown to the warmth, and the endless stretch of blue sky is rarely broken by clouds. The few cypress trees and palms only add to the oppressiveness of the light, for their yellow-green is overpowered until it becomes almost the color of the sun. Still one cannot resist raising one's eyes to have a look at the Acropolis rising on its long battlements just a half mile to the left above the Plaza. There the broken columns of the Parthenon stand in wounded dignity against the sky, giving a splendid impression of the colors which make Greece—gold and blue.

Standing for a moment in the lobby of the Hotel Mediterranean Plaza, I blinked to adjust my eyes to the dusky interior. It was then that I heard Costas laugh. His laughter was full, not raucous like that of most Greek boys, and somewhat humble as befits an elevator boy, as though he were expecting you to laugh with him. I noticed his long rows of teeth, shining and perfect, and his wide mouth. His face was broad to begin with, and his laughter pushed his cheeks out even farther. His black hair, brilliant and thick, was brushed back over his head in the pompadour style which used to be so popular among American boys. He must have been about fifteen at the time, but because of his stocky build he appeared more mature than his age—a kind of man and boy in one. I never did learn the cause of his laughter that morning; I merely looked at him with a half smile and accepted his courtesies as he asked my floor and let me off the elevator with those effusive "sirs" by which the Greeks show politeness.

But I noticed a book opened and turned upside down on his elevator chair, the *Dramas of Sophocles*. Later as I sat in my room writing, gazing out into the shaded patio at the rear of the hotel, I thought how Costas resembled my own younger brother back in America. Except the reading of Sophocles—I marveled at that.

It would have surprised me to know then that this laughing boy would in a few years be picking his way through the fir trees of Albanian mountains, holding a rifle with bayonet gleaming as he led a suicide squad against an Italian outpost.

### The Forced Migration

One evening, two weeks later, I came across him sitting on a bench in the Plaza, and I heard a story which has remained deeply etched in my memory ever since. I sat down beside him, partly because I was curious to learn more about this boy and partly because I wished to enjoy the refreshing loveliness of the evening. Summer evenings in Athens, when for two hours after sundown the sky plays with shades of pink and turquoise, can be as invigorating as the days are stifling. A languid breeze comes up from the Bay of Salamis, loaded with rich fragrance which has been accumulating in the drying, semi-tropical vegetation on the island of Aegina several miles out in the bay. The breeze brings with it an occasional pungent odor from the harbor of the Piraeus. Music seems to carry farther on such an evening, and the sporadic taxi horns did not clash too cacophonously with the tango music emerging from a restaurant at the far end of the Plaza. I had often sat on this bench, letting myself be lulled by the lazy movement of palm fingers moving in and out of the darkness above my head, then turning to watch the lights come on way up Mt. Lycabettus. I often counted the stars as they sprang out with a brilliance possible only in the transparent atmosphere of Mediterranean countries.

Costas had been reading a book before the sun had set, and he answered my question about what he was reading with his irrepressible laugh that accompanied every utterance, humorous or not.

"The history, sir, of the Persian Wars, sir."

That curious "sir" twice in one sentence! It did seem to me that they overdid their courtesy.

"You find it interesting?"

"O yes sir, yes sir! One of my ancestors fought at Thermopylae. His name was Argyros, and he was a very brave man."

"You don't believe, Costas, that the ancient Greeks who fought those Persians were the same race as the modern Greeks, do you?" I baited him.

"O yes, yes sir!" he cried earnestly, using the word *malista* which carries a strong affirmation like our English *certainly.* "I come from Asia Minor," he went on so quickly that he stammered, "from Asia Minor, sir, the Ionian Greeks lived there, and they are the descendants directly from the Greeks who fought at Thermopylae."

"How did they get over to Asia Minor?"

"The people of the Peloponnesus, sir, migrated to Asia Minor. Our family lived in the Peloponnesus in ancient times. My great ancestor went with the Spartan army under Leonidas to fight at Thermopylae. He was one of the three hundred who stayed to hold the pass for three days so they would have time to fortify Athens. He died there. My father often told me about our

84

ancestor Argyros. Then many years later the Greeks from the Peloponnesus made a colony in Asia Minor."

Costas was spouting this history like a religious faith. I knew it was fairly dubious—modern Greeks are mainly Slavic in race, and historians don't know where the glorious race of the ancient Hellenes ended. But I saw there was no use arguing ethnology with the zealous Costas, and furthermore I did want to pump him about himself.

"Does your father still live in Asia Minor?"

"No sir, he was killed by the Turks." Costas said it calmly, as though he had uttered that sentence so often it had become just a statement of objective fact to him.

"I'm sorry. When was that?"

"In the massacres of 1922. Almost every Greek in our town was killed. You do not know, sir, about those massacres?"

I did know something of the war between Turkey and Greece in 1922, which ended with the terrible battle of Smyrna when the city was burned, and the Greek army with thousands of refugees was driven right into the sea and would have been annihilated, had it not been for the timely aid of some British warships that picked up those who could swim or get hold of boats. But evidently Costas was thinking of something else.

"We lived in the town of Merzifoun, way back near the Caucasus. I was a small boy then, but I remember the town well. Almost all the people were Greeks—the only Turks around were government officials. They didn't bother us much and we had a happy life. My father used to ride about the country on horseback buying tobacco to sell to American companies. He sometimes took me riding with him on his trips—I would sit on the old horse behind him. There weren't many towns in our province, you see, only barren hills and plateaus.

"When we arrived in a village the men were always glad to see my father. They would take him to the café and sit at the tables in the street and drink Turkish coffee and a little ouzo and laugh and talk. These were Greeks, sir, the Turks in the village would stand around without ever smiling; they always seemed sour at something. But my father got along with them well, he never quarreled with them, and he used to greet them cheerfully and offer them cigarettes. The Turks would sit at their own café, never talking or laughing like my father and his friends, only silently smoking their long waterpipes. I used to sit at the edge of the street a little way from my father's table and watch those Turks smoking. Have you seen those Turkish pipes, sir?"

"Yes," I answered. Then I added, "You must have been very fond of your father."

"I loved him very much," said Costas. The boy was now sitting moodily, looking out across the Plaza toward the sparkling lights on Mt. Lycabettus, and he went on talking not as an elevator boy to an *Amerikanos* but as one human being to another.

"The happiest memories of my whole life are those trips I took with my father. Oh, we had good enough times at home, my mother and two sisters and I. But how I loved to go with my father! As we were riding the many hours between villages he would tell me stories of the ancient Greeks, how the Persians came down with a huge army and the Athenians fought them at Marathon and drove them into the sea and killed so many that the mound where they are buried looks like a mountain. And he told me about Leonidas the Spartan general who made the stand at Thermopylae. That was when my father would speak about Argyros, our great ancestor. I used to be so filled with pride I almost burst when I heard how my ancestor had volunteered to stay with the three hundred soldiers in the narrow pass in the mountains, and how he fought there even though the Persian arrows were so thick they hid the sun. Then my father would tell me about the shepherd traitor who took the Persians around by a secret pass to attack Leonidas and the Spartans from the rear, and my anger would boil up and my father would laugh as I clenched my fists. But he was proud that I begged to hear those stories over and over again. And he used to say, 'Costaki, never forget that your great ancestor was Argyros'."

The boy was talking animatedly now, his hands gesturing aimlessly around in the dark. In the dim lights of the Plaza lamps I got a glimpse of his black eyes dancing with delight at these boyhood memories. But suddenly he sat quietly, vacantly, his face sober and his jaw heavily set.

"Your mother and sisters," I ventured, "did they come to Greece with you?"

"My sister Ismene did. The Turks took the older one, and my mother died on the exile."

I had heard something about this dramatic exile. The Turks had endeavored to end the problem of the Greek and Armenian minorities within their borders once and for all after the battle of Smyrna by moving thousands of people in a gigantic caravan from one end of Asia Minor to the other.

"One day the Turkish soldiers came to our town," Costas went on, "and announced that everyone had to get ready to move. My father was surprised and desperate, but he and most of the other Greeks had learned during the war not to talk back. Two men who did object were shot in the village square—that made people move faster in their packing. We didn't know where we were going, so it was hard to tell what to take along. My father loaded a cart and harnessed our horse to it, and we started out well enough riding. There were hundreds in that straggling line—all our village—the men were trudging along through the dust carrying sacks, the women were dragging children by the hands and some girls were carrying their baby brothers and sisters. The Turkish soldiers rode on horses on each side of the line, and if anyone moved too slowly they cursed and pushed the person along with a stick.

"The first night we slept out we could see the sky red where our village was burning. It was hot during the day—there aren't many shade trees on those plateaus. After three days' march the people began to get sick and fall down around us. My father and the other men were filled with rage, but they couldn't do anything, there were too many soldiers and they had sabers and pistols. At first the soldiers behaved pretty well— the government had given orders to carry out the exile as orderly as possible. But after a few days they began to make insulting remarks to the girls in the line, and they whipped one old man who fell down with exhaustion in the middle of the day.

"When we had been on the trail about a week my mother got sick. The Turks had taken our horse away, and my mother and sisters and I were walking and my father was pulling the cart. I noticed my mother was white that morning, but she kept her face stiff and walked on. You couldn't tell how people felt because nobody dared to talk. It was a very hot day, and in the afternoon my mother suddenly fell down in a heap. I've thought about it afterwards—a heat stroke, I guess. They buried her right there. The next two days my father plodded on with his head down, saying nothing at all, and looking like a man I had never known.

"Then the Turks took my sister, Helene. She was a lot older than I, and she was beautiful—everyone in our village used to say that. The soldiers had been getting more and more rough, and that night they took my sister and some other girls out of the camp. She screamed and kicked but they struck her and held their hands over her mouth. Most of the soldiers went off and we could hear their singing and yelling during the night around their fire a few miles away.

"That night my father did not sleep. I heard him crawl away from the place where Ismene and I were lying. I lay stiff and afraid all night long, and I finally heard some soldiers coming back to relieve those who had been guarding us. They were drunk. Just as it began to get light my father crawled back and I could hear him whispering to Ismene. Then he was gone.

"Suddenly we heard shots and shouting and Turkish curses. We jumped up and we could see men running. My father and some of the other men had stolen the pistols and sabers of the drunken guards. They had killed every guard that had been stationed around us, and then they ran over behind some bags piled in the field. The other Turkish soldiers came back and there was shooting from every side. I began to cry and tried to run to my father. Ismene held me back. But I broke away and ran across the field. The men were crouched in a circle, they weren't shooting anymore, it seems their pistols were empty. But they had a few sabers among them, and they knelt behind their bags waiting for the soldiers to come on. It was only a dozen or so of our men—they knew they'd get killed, and I guess the others were afraid or else they couldn't get weapons so they stayed back. The Turkish soldiers were gathering in a large outer circle, swearing and shouting."

Costas stopped for a moment. Then he went on in a low voice, "My father was lying on the ground with blood over his shirt. His face was white. I fell down beside him and he smiled a little. 'Costaki,' I heard him say, 'We are of Argyros.' The Turks came rushing on, I remember sabers clashing right over my head. Then suddenly things became quiet. I clung to my father's body crying like a baby, but a soldier jerked me away."

In the pause I was scarcely conscious of the tango music from the far end of the plaza. Taxi horns whining out of the darkness did not break the mood his story had created. I tried to suggest a more comforting lead, "You say this other sister, Ismene, came to Greece with you?"

"We both came on the ship. The League of Nations had a shipload of orphans brought to Athens. But my sister got pneumonia in the refugee camp in Piraeus and died there."

I knew no other hopeful leads, so I was silent too. I sensed he was crying but I didn't turn to look. He must have felt the discomfort of the silence himself, for in a few moments he stood up.

"Excuse me, sir. It's late, I must go."

After he had left I lit a cigarette and watched the palms play a game of hide-and-seek with the stars. When

I finally arose to go in I saw he had forgotten his *History of the Persian Wars.*

When I gave him his book on the elevator in the morning his smile was as irresistible as when I had first met him. Now, of course, I knew the secret of his perpetual optimism—it was the buoyancy of a person who had suffered greatly but was glad to be alive. One living with memories like his would have to develop the ability to laugh long and well, or else be engulfed in despair.

A stroke of luck came to Costas six months later. Mr. Cornelius Sheffield, a director of the Associated Press, was visiting me in Athens. Sheffield was attracted as I had been by the spectacle of an elevator boy reading Sophocles, so he decided to send Costas on to school. The boy was anxious to go, and they selected the American University at Saloniki.

I heard during the next couple of years that Costas was doing well. Evidently his buoyancy was popular with his fellow-students, for he was elected president of his class, and he had become a leading all-round student of the University.

Then in 1935 I was transferred to Istanbul and lost track of him. We newspaper men lead a roving life—I was next in Sophia and then Belgrade. And in September, 1940 I was sent back to Athens.

Just in time, too, for the press wires suddenly became hot with activity. The Italian army had come swelling like a flood into northern Greece. Through the Albanian passes rolled the tanks and troops, and Mussolini boasted that he would inundate Epirus in three weeks and have his legions marching triumphantly through the streets of Saloniki like the ancient Roman Galerius.

General Metaxas ordered full mobilization and the papers carried his clarion call all over the country: "Greeks, we shall now prove whether we are worthy of our ancestors and of the liberty which our forefathers secured for us!"

But the news from the front caused only despair. Rumor had it that a fully equipped division of Italian Alpini had pushed down through the valley of the Pindus Mountains and was already pounding tanks into Metsovan. To drive the discouragement home, Italian bombers growled over Athens, pausing to bark over the airport at Tatoi until it resembled the nearby stone quarries gashing the slopes of Pentelicus. Two bombs burst in the crowded port of Piraeus sending half a block of little white and pink houses into a cloud of pulverized mortar. Athenian citizens were panicky, and they gathered in little knots on the streets gesturing so nervously that it was impossible to unravel any coherent emotion from their talk except the insistent cry, "When will the *Angloi* come? Where are the *Anglikos* warships?"

We American newspaper men who harbored a warm affection for Greece and its people were filled with anxiety. We could not pretend to be optimistic as we thought of the poorly-trained Greek soldiers trying to stand up against the mechanized military steamroller of the north.

But suddenly news of a different sort broke on the wires. Could the rumor be true that the Greeks cut off a whole Italian division in the Pindus Valley? Was it possible that Metaxas' *evzones*—as the honor guards were called—had broken up the conflict into separate combat, in which the sheer heroic enthusiasm of individual

92

Greeks could tear and bite at the fabric of the Italian Alpini until it split into pieces?

The church bells of Athens rang out in joyful frenzy as report after report of Greek victory came in over the wires. The enemy was in full retreat, sang the newspaper headlines. Citizens who had been weighted down by a funereal mood two weeks earlier now lost themselves in ecstasy as they paraded down the streets of the capitol, and myriads of blue and white flags leaped from every pole in the city.

Newspapers in Athens began to use the words _Thermopylae_ and _Marathon_ and _Leonides_. So that was it! The inspiration of the courage of the ancient Greeks was running like a forest fire over the mountaintops where the Greek _evzones_ were pushing back Mussolini's troops. And I remembered Costas Argyropoulos and his zealous faith in his ancestor of ancient Hellas.

_Heroes and Heroism_

It was a month after the war had started that I heard of Costas again. The Italians were entirely out of Greece by that time—Kastoria and the border towns were in Greek hands and Saloniki was safe. The army was chasing the enemy from Porto Edda to the accompaniment of the cheers from the democratic world. The papers in America clamored for human interest stories to fill in the blanks of our previously sketchy military communications. I heard that a lieutenant who had commanded one of the crucial sectors in the battle of the Pindus Valley was in the Athenian Military Hospital on the slopes of Mt. Hymmetus to the south of Athens, so I went to see him in quest of a story.

Lieutenant Pararas was not wounded badly; he had

to keep off his right leg. But we were able to sit on the
hospital porch and look down the gentle slope of Hymmetus to the great crescent of little white and pink tinted
houses of Athens. This view of the city often reminded
me of a shovelful of little hard candies thrown on the
slope, barely escaping rolling down into the blue bay.

Lieutenant Pararas was a cultured, gentle person,
middle-aged and handsome with his black eyes and hair.
He conversed in delightful English with an Oxford touch.
Before the invasion he had been a teacher in the American University of Saloniki, I learned, and his command
had been made up mainly of young men from that school.
The fact that grasped my attention most sharply was
that Costas Argyropoulos had been in his command.

"Our soldiers exhibit a remarkable bravery," said
Pararas in a mild well-modulated voice. He was a most
un-military individual, and if it had not been for his
khaki uniform and his bandaged foot I should not have
believed he was a lieutenant. After obtaining enough
firsthand material for my story, I inquired about Costas.

"What a surprise that you know Argyropoulos!" he
cried. "He was a splendid young man. He did more to
keep up the morale of my troops than I could myself.
He was always laughing, even when we had to stand for
two days in a drift of snow." The lieutenant smiled at
me, then his face became sober. "Argyropoulos was killed
in that advance."

I said nothing, leaving the way open for Pararas to
proceed.

"He volunteered for the most difficult venture of the
whole Pindus campaign. Our advance was blocked by

an outpost of Italians in a monastery which was situated on a ledge on the perpendicular face of the mountain. The monastery—Hagia Sophia, perhaps you are acquainted with it?—was inaccessible except by one narrow circuitous route from below, barely wide enough for a line of men. The Italians had sent a squad up this path to take the monastery, and had then drawn their guns up by the cable and windlass the monks had constructed for drawing up their own supplies. The Italians had fortified the place well, and they could have blown us to bits if we had advanced down the valley. We couldn't go around the fort either; the mountain peaks in that section are too difficult to permit transporting any guns whatever. And we couldn't bomb the Italians out, for they had kept the monks of the monastery there, and every hour they forced them at gunpoint to march up and down the walls as a sign to our troops that shelling the monastery would mean killing the monks. Our people have a great veneration for their monks; there was no suggestion that we bombard the fortification. But General Melitus dared not advance to the north of us until this valley was taken, so he sent orders to clean the Italians out of that monastery.

"I called for volunteers—a dozen of them I thought might be able to climb down the face of the rock from above, surprise the Italians in the monastery, and cause enough damage to put their fort out of activity.

"Costas Argyropoulos was the first to step forward," the lieutenant continued. "But he looked curiously different from the Argyropoulos we had grown to know. I suppose one should expect a soldier to appear sober when he volunteers for almost certain death. But I was none the less surprised at this fellow who had kept us all laughing for two weeks now facing me with as serious and immovable expression as the mountain itself."

I nodded, remembering how Costas had once unintentionally proved to me that old truth that the persons who appear most buoyant on the surface often reach down into the most profound depths underneath.

That night Costas had led the little line of volunteers up through the forest to the mountain ridge. They carried only pistols and sabers, for rifles would have gotten snagged in the thick brush through which they had to push their way to the top, and any other arms would have made too dangerous the difficult descent on the mountain face down to the ledge. I knew well how inaccessible these monasteries were. Though I had never visited Hagia Sophia, I had spent one Easter vacation climbing and riding mule-back through Meteora, a group of monasteries on the other side of this Pindus range. The monks themselves had been hospitable enough, but their holy retreats were always perched on some isolated ledge to remove them as far as possible from the commerce of the world below. So successful was this isolation that in many cases the only way to get into the little communities was by being hauled up in a basket, with the bearded, black-gowned old monks grinding the creaking windlass above you as you came up. Evidently Hagia Sophia enjoyed an almost ideal location—from the point of view of saints or enemy soldiers.

"Costas and his men picked their way down the face of the rock," continued the lieutenant, "and about an hour before dawn they were lying above the inside monastery wall which came directly out of the mountain."

96

One of the survivors of the little party later told Lieutenant Pararas that the men wanted to leap immediately into the courtyard and attack the garrison by starlight, but Costas ordered them to wait motionless.

Then two monks came along the wall. These holy men had learned the practice of arising and praying at three in the morning—a habit imbued through so many generations that even in times of enemy occupation they felt compelled to get up and prowl toward the chapel in the attempt to fulfill their accustomed duty. This practice was, this morning, an answer to the Greek soldiers' prayer. The soft footsteps and the rustle of the gowns came closer. Huge black forms loomed up. A hissing whisper from Argyropoulos and the black figures stopped.

Costas crawled down upon the top of the wall, and the whispering continued. The monks then guided the volunteers down into the courtyard itself.

By this time just the slightest light was diffused in the dawn and the rooms which were part of the four walls of this miniature medieval town dimly gave way into the darkness on either side. Looming vaguely in the center of the courtyard fifty yards away was the chapel. Costas instructed his men where the sentries were posted and where the main body of the garrison was sleeping, and the Greeks crawled away to their tasks. Fifteen minutes later when it was light enough to see from one end of the courtyard to the other, the figures of the five sentries could be discerned on the outer wall. They came down in a file at the corner where the Greeks crouched. The Greeks leapt with their sabers, and three of the sentries went down with hardly more sound than a gulp.

But the other two Italians broke away and ran across the courtyard. The pistols cracked and one twisted on his heel like a child dizzy from too much whirling, and fell over on his side. Costas quickly stationed his men behind strategic windows and waited for the garrison. He had figured that there must be at least thirty men behind the windows at the far end. The plan was to bluff it out coolly on the hunch that the Italians would greatly overestimate the size of the attacking party and give up rather than fight it out. So far in the war the Italians had often shown their lack of desire to martyr themselves; their hearts and their homes were not in this conflict.

Lieutenant Pararas and his troops in the valley below peered up intently at the monastery when they heard the pistol shots. As dawn shed a growing light into the valley and the vast expanse of rock above was being bathed in rosy hues, they could see the walls of the tiny holy city, set like a toy clinging to the bare face of the mountain. Above the monastery walls the round dome of the chapel yearned upward, its red and white brick shining in the sun. The flashing of the sunlight upon the cross which crowned the dome made the church look like a lighthouse, a holy port sheltered by the impregnable rock of the mountain. But this morning the peaceful appearance of the monastery was quite deceptive. The sacred beauty of Hagia Sophia was scarcely congruous with that repeated, spasmodic sound of pistol shots.

Then there was silence above. Pararas strained nervously, trying to bear the heavy moments of uncertainty. After a quarter of an hour the gates of the monastery swung open, and the eager lieutenant saw emerging the strangest clerical procession that had ever taken place in those mountains. The monks filed out of the gate and down the path, their black gowns swishing as they hurried from their retreat which had become the enemy's fort. Their black hats, stuck upon their heads like elongated inverted cans, bobbed to and fro as they moved steadily and quickly around the belly of rock.

After the score of monks came two of the Greek soldiers, and behind them the line of captured enemies, empty-handed, some without hats, many with the unbuttoned coats of their green uniforms flapping. Pararas kept count as the uninspiring party of surrendered men filed out, thirty-two of them altogether. And finally a few yards behind the last Italian appeared the khaki uniforms of the other Greeks.

The soldiers looking up from the valley let out a cheer which bounded to the face of the mountain and echoed back. There was no telling whether the long procession heard it. The line of the monks and soldiers continued to edge along the mountainside, twisting and cutting back here and there as the dangerous path tried to hold its own against the hostile rock which seemed ready to push it over the precipice.

But the cheering suddenly stopped. The rapid tat-tat-tat of a machine-gun came from the monastery. The Greeks at the end of the line stood etched against the stone. The monks, now safely around the belly of the cliff, began to run, holding their skirts up to their knees. The prisoners hesitated for a moment but they moved on as part of the Greek guard pushed them with drawn pistols.

Lieutenant Pararas stared anxiously up the mountain. Four of the Greek guard remained motionless, looking back toward the monastery. The telegraphic clicking of the machine-gun was repeated, and one of the khaki uniforms collapsed.

Evidently the troops in the valley and the men above grasped the situation at about the same instant. In every monastery there are many rooms where ancient Bibles and manuscripts are stored. These rooms are dark and dusty; many of them are not entered from year to year, and occasionally the monks have lost the keys so the rooms sit empty except for their treasure. The Italians had been more clever than Argyropoulos anticipated; they had left a handful of men in a secluded attic which the searching party of the Greeks had not penetrated. Now they manned a machine-gun and had command of the path for a hundred yards below the gate.

When one of his party fell, Costas ordered the rest of his men around the belly of the rock with a quick gesture. But his stocky figure remained still against the mountain. Pararas was almost beside himself with excitement, "Come down! Come down!" he shouted, as though some magic wind or mental telepathy would carry his words to the figure high above.

But Costas moved cautiously back toward the monastery. By leaping from boulder to boulder he made progress, while the machine-gun spat and swore, and chips of rock leaped from under his feet. Occasionally a bullet careened off the mountain and sang across the valley in a drunken hum.

Lieutenant Pararas began to moan, "Oh, why doesn't he come down?" They could blast the monastery to kingdom come now that the monks were out. But Costas was evidently of another mind. The khaki spot clung for a moment against the belly of the rock, then leapt suddenly to the protection of the next boulder. The machine-gun spat again. But the figure alternately crouched low on the path or crawled or jumped to cling behind the next protrusion of rock. Whether the machine-gun was poorly placed or whether Costas utilized the boulders so effectively that he could not be hit will never be known. But he reached the protection of the wall, ran down it twenty feet and through the gate. The pistol shots were the last sounds Pararas and his men heard from the monastery. The squad which went up later in the morning found the body of Costas with those of the three dead machine-gunners. He had saved the spiritual and physical beauty of the monastery with his death.

"The government sent his body to Saloniki and he will be buried there with full honors," the lieutenant concluded. After a moment he offered his military summary, "Well, we got through. It was in our advance the next day that the entire Italian Alpini division was captured."

I looked out past the pillars of the porch of the military hospital, down the easy slope of Hymmetus and across the city of Athens to the acropolis where I could just make out the broken columns of the Parthenon, sunny and brave against the deep blue of the bay of Salamis several miles beyond.

I made a mental note to look up in the Athenian papers the citation of Costas Argyropoulos. I doubted whether the government would see any connection between this young man and the minor hero of a similar name who died in a similarly rash way at Thermopylae.

But I couldn't resist the temptation to make an intentional error in my report to my own paper. I would write his name Costas Argyros, for I knew that was the way he thought of it.

# CHAPTER VI

# A City
## SET ON A Hill

*The citizens of the City of God*
*use spiritual weapons—*
*prayer and love and truth.*
*The City of God is heaven,*
*but its splendor comes into the City of the World*
*in the truth and love which finally*
*will conquer even the sword.*

SAINT AUGUSTINE

# 6

*A Marriage Banquet in Larissa*

HILEMON LIFTED his arm so that the dangling black sleeve of his monk's gown would not drag in the food on the table, and turned to his brother:

"By all the saints in heaven, Giorgos, she is beautiful!"

Giorgos looked up the long banquet table, over the stubby forest of wine glasses between the ridges of chattering guests, to his bride-to-be sitting at the head of the table.

"Surely," he answered fervently, and in typically Greek overstatement, "the most beautiful woman in the world!"

Hypatia's black hair was shining under the light hanging above her head. Her white lace gown, only half covering shapely shoulders, made her look like the queen of the celebration—which of course she was. She presented a contrast in black and white: the natural paleness of her skin—the olive complexion of the Greeks it has been called—made whiter by the excitement of the occasion. Her jet black eyes, large and oval, flashed when she looked up to smile at some newly arrived guests bowing before her with their effusive felicitations. Her rich, full breasts trembled under the tight white gown. Her lips were a brilliant crimson, giving a gleaming spot of color to bring alive the white and the shining blackness.

But Hypatia looked frightened. Like the glow of a firefly, her fugitive smile beamed and vanished. Most of the time she had been sitting there—and it had been since sundown till now, almost midnight—she had looked down demurely into the glass of champagne before her, trying to find some release in this fairy-land of sparkle. Some of the excitement came from the attention bestowed upon her, some from the tingling sensations accompanying her glances at Giorgos at the far end of the banquet table. But most of her fright came from the bewildering anticipation of marrying a man she scarcely knew.

Oh, she had seen him often enough. He had come to her home regularly on Sundays, and had amused the circle of her family with stories about the peasants in the mountains of Thrace, from whom he bought tobacco for his father to ship to America. The peasants thought half of America was made up of stone pavement and the other half of wild Indians. But she had never been alone with him for more than a moment. Marriages are arranged by parents in Greece, following a custom hallowed by age and blessed with fair success.

She knew she loved him; whenever he had been near her during the past months she felt herself turning hot and cold at the same instant. And when he left she could scarcely wait to get to bed where she could lie looking up in the darkness and reconstructing in her imagination his smooth features, as though she were running her hand through his hair. And now as the moment for giving herself completely to him approached, her fright made him seem suddenly a stranger.

As guests continued to come in, Hypatia's father met them at the door with a torrent of words of welcome, for the Greeks are most of all loquacious. Here was Colonel Theodorides, tall and stiff in his khaki uniform, on leave from the front on the Struma river a hundred miles to the north. His massive face did not relax as he bowed before Hypatia and marched to a seat at the end of the table near Giorgos. And here was Kyrie Gounaris, the principal of the gymnasium, who had been proud of his diploma from the University of Berlin until the armies of the Nazis had begun to gather in Bulgaria a month earlier. And there was Iatrides, the apothecary who owned the drug shop on the corner.

Giorgos, occupying an incidental position near the foot of the table as befits the unimportant groom, was an exuberant young man whose glance went actively about the room even while he conversed out of the corner of his mouth with his brother. Both he and Philemon had the smoothly carved features which are the last remaining vestige of the physique of the ancient Greeks. But Giorgos' face was heavier than his brother's, and his broad shoulders and actively curly hair would have earned him the description of "athletic" in America. He smiled gaily as he looked from side to side.

"Of course she is beautiful, my Philemon," using that strange possessive form in talking to a close relative. "Why do you think I've been coming down here every week for a year? And you, my dear brother, would be marrying an Aphrodite just as exquisite if you hadn't chosen this black gown instead." He dangled the sleeve of Philemon's monastic habit.

Somewhat taller, Philemon was a year older than his brother. His nose came smoothly down from his forehead in classic style, and he had that rarity around the Mediterranean, blue eyes with black hair. He did not mind his brother's joking about his having become a novice in the monastery at twenty-one, two years earlier, for he knew that Giorgos was secretly proud of the fact.

"You are fortunate, Giorgaki," he answered. "You'll be very happy. Be sure to take good care of her, or you'll have me to answer to."

"Stop!" Giorgos laughed, clapping his brother on the knee. "One would think you were envious of me! By the sacred Mary, there isn't a girl in Larissa who hasn't been secretly in love with you, and, from what I hear, at the University in Athens as well. How you could stay innocent so long is a miracle to me. No doubt that's what love of books does for you!"

"Some men are made for marriage with a woman," said Philemon, gazing meditatively into the glass of water he played with between his slender fingers. "But some of us are made to marry a faith—just as the colonel here has married a flag."

108

"Perhaps we'll all have to leave our wives for that flag." Giorgos' face had suddenly become darkly clouded. "That's what I fear, my Philemon. Promise me—promise me as your brother," he implored, "if the Germans attack and I don't come back from the Struma, will you take care of Hypatia?"

"Believe me, I will! But let us hope in God's name they leave our nation free."

"Colonel Theodorides!" called Giorgos above the chatter around him, "what is the news from Saloniki?"

The colonel had been drinking ouzo, the whitish liqueur flavored with anise seed. The little glass was barely the thickness of his two massive fingers. He had been sitting, so unlike a Greek, in silence. Perhaps that is what crawling over Albanian peaks—attacking, retreating and attacking again—had done to him.

"They'll come," he stated simply. "The sergeants at Saloniki say they already have two thousand tanks at the Struma pass."

"Then we'll fight!" cried Giorgos. "We can die as well as our fathers! We'll fight if ten thousand tanks come through!"

The moustache of Iatrides, the apothecary sitting next to Giorgos, trembled as he stuttered nervously. "We surprised the world in Albania! We'll hold them again!" Everyone at the table was thinking of Marathon and Thermopylae in this history the Greeks loved so much.

The loud voices of several Greeks, which became inflamed like fuses when their nation's honor was at stake, made a confusion of the conversation. Out of the melee came the voice of the teacher, Gounaris.

"We'll die if need be. But the Germans are formidable. Is it possible to hold them, Colonel?"

"In the army· we cannot ask that," shouted the colonel above the hubbub. "They are formidable, yes. But we fight—we fight and die—it is all, perhaps. Papas Philemon, pray for us. In God's name, let all the monasteries pray!"

"Yes, they will pray for us," cried Giorgos, "they who do not believe in fighting! But what we need is soldiers to man the guns! Every patriotic Greek must fight in the crisis!"

The group was suddenly quiet, sensing the offense to their church. Giorgos saw the hurt in his brother's face. The anger on his own softened. This was an old argument between the brothers—Giorgos the active one, to whom the flag was the highest symbol of devotion and who sought no higher glory than to spill his blood beneath that cloth of blue and white; and Philemon the thoughtful, who even as a boy in the gymnasium had pondered for hours about a spiritual force stronger than firearms.

"But if the soul of Greece," said Philemon, "is not kept alive, what will there be to fight for?"

"That is right," eagerly spoke Gounaris. "The monasteries kept the soul of our country alive under the oppression by the Turks. They taught us to love the heroism of our fathers regardless of how much we must sacrifice for it."

Giorgos put his arm on his brother's shoulder. "Forgive my anger, my Philemon. But when I think that I shall be married and then perhaps shall die—immediately. . . ."

"But no sorrow here," cried Iatrides with effort. "It is your wedding, son! Here, a toast to Hellas, and then only joy!"

The delicate bowls of champagne chimed again, "To Hellas, the land of our fathers!" Tears rolled down the cheeks of the apothecary. The colonel's jaw clamped solidly, and the eyes of the others glistened as they sang the national anthem,

I recognize you from the terrible cut of the sword. . . .
You who have risen from the sacred bones of the Greeks,
And as strong and brave as you were of old,
We salute you!

It was two o'clock in the morning, and the remaining hours till dawn were spent in gladness and in eating and drinking and affectionate felicitations on all sides. When the dawn painted the windows with a purple light, Giorgos kissed his brother farewell and Philemon kissed Hypatia. Amid tears mainly of joy Giorgos and his bride left by taxi for Volos, the little village clinging to the side of Mount Pelion where lovers can sit by the hour and watch the blue-green water, clear as glass, sighing against the pink rocks of the mountain.

*The Country One Loves*

Philemon rode in the little narrow-gauge train that chugged up the valley and across the plains from Larissa to Trikkala. The shiny steam-engine, no higher than a man, breathed efficiently as it pulled its baby-cars. It could well be efficient, Philemon knew, for it was made in Germany. Philemon relaxed and looked out on the April countryside, squared with the damp green of spring wheat. Here a peasant stopped his ploughing to watch the train go by. He waved to Philemon, leaning on the quaint handle of his wooden plough while his huge water

Street in Kalambaka, April '33

buffalo bent its giant head and long horns near the soil as though sniffing a trail for the plough.

A little farther on a farmer was plodding along behind his donkey loaded so high with brush that only four stiff ankles of the animal could be seen. The three children strung behind the farmer waved hankerchiefs as Philemon and the train went by. They are going to that school down the road, and they come from that hut of mud bricks over there, thought Philemon. How homey a scene! How typical of my country!

After two hours ride from Larissa, Philemon saw looming up ahead the high fingers of rock upon which his monastery was perched. The range of the Pindus mountains in central Greece meets the back of Mount Olympus in a gap which is toothed by these strange high formations of rock. Called Meteora—meaning the middle of the air—the rocks rear up like giant leaning towers of Pisa. Time was when the only way to get up to the monastery perched on top was the huge basket attached by cable to the windlass above, which the monks would turn after making sure the passengers were fellow-monks or supplies. This is why, it is said, the Turks never conquered Meteora when they subdued the rest of Greece in the seventeenth century.

Philemon began his climb up the path which curved round the base of this finger of rock like spiral steps up a light house. He paused after several minutes to catch his breath and look out over the valley. Off to the left, where the green squares of spring wheat began, a Judas tree stood in full bloom, throwing up its delicately flaming pink like the opening notes in a joyous paean to spring. Below and to the right, where the soil swung up to meet the base of the rock, a blanket of crimson

113

poppies wove back and forth in the breeze, alive and vibrant. The rich red flowers were so dense that Philemon could not catch a glimpse of green for a hundred yards—it was an intoxicating drink of pure color.

Philemon breathed in the scene with delight.

"Ah, Greece!" he cried aloud. "The Hellas of our father! How abundantly God has spread his beauty here!" His spirit soared with happiness, and in his exuberance he broke into a run along the path, which now zig-zagged up the bare face of rock.

An hour's walk brought him to the top where the great wooden door, ribbed with rusty iron, gave an opening in the stone walls. The monks were just going across the courtyard to supper. Here was Papas Demetrikos, the abbot of the monastery, whose gown flowed in his wake as he walked briskly over the cobble-stones. His black hat was clamped down over his long white hair, which curved round his face and into his full beard to make a wide frame for this face.

*"Kalespera,* my son," he said shaking hands with Philemon warmly, "Thanks to God you are safely returned. And just at the hour for food."

The twenty or so monks sat round a bare wooden table in the refectory. It was a dull room with scant light from the late afternoon falling through the high windows, illuminating some of the verses from the holy writings painted on the walls. But the conversation was more jolly than the surroundings. Michaelides, a young novice from Philemon's class at the University of Athens, pumped him for information about the wedding, and the other monks listened eagerly. Though no women were allowed on top of this finger of rock, the monks were actively amused as Philemon described the beauty of his new sister-in-law.

114

The cook shuffled in with the food—bean soup, lettuce, fish and brown bread which looked like hard-packed sawdust and tasted slightly sour. Across from Philemon sat a Jesuit, a famous scholar from America, who wore a white hood over his gown. He had been a guest in the monastery for six months, and every day he spent long hours in the library pouring over the precious old manuscripts, which, at the fancy of some copyist of long ago, had gold letters brightly trimmed in blue with quaint red birds painted in the corners of the pages.

When the supper was half over one of the monks stood up. It was the dignified Papas Stavrou, whom Philemon reverenced as one of the great theologians of his church. The reading this evening was from Saint Augustine.

"The City of God is above the City of the World," came Papas Stavrou's precise yet sing-songish voice. "The City of the World goes down to destruction as the proud pillars of Rome were overturned. The armies of the City of the World fight with swords and spears, but the words of our blessed Lord are true, 'They that take the sword shall perish by the sword.' The citizens of the City of God use spiritual weapons—prayer and love and truth. The City of God is heaven, but its splendor comes into the City of the World in the truth and love which finally will conquer even the sword."

After supper Philemon wandered out upon the grassy table-land which stretched for several acres on the top of this tower of rock. The sun was setting behind the farthest Pindus ridge, and the grass at his feet glowed alight with the reflection from the orange sky. He lay on the grass at the edge of the rock, looking down into the blank gray space of a quarter of a mile to the shining outline of the river in the valley. Sheep must have been making their way toward that cluster of huts in the village, for he heard the faint tinkle of bells echoing up this ridge. The evening breeze which touched his skin with coolness brought the perfume of wisteria.

"This heavenly peace!" he murmured. "Is this the City of God?" Then he remembered that the Italian army had almost broken into this quiet valley six months before. He shook off the thought as too ugly to be harbored.

In his musing he remembered Hypatia. Her oval black eyes glowed suddenly in his memory. He was filled with a delicious pleasure. She seemed to fit into this twilight atmosphere. He was bouyant as he walked back in the deepening darkness to his room.

As he lay in bed images of Hypatia came tumbling down on all sides, engulfing him. She had seemed frightened at the wedding, he remembered. Her breasts had trembled as she breathed. He had yearned to put his arm around her shoulder, to protect her, to care for her. To love a girl like Hypatia would indeed be a joy. Men of the world possessed such women. It seemed too wonderful to be true, and Philemon was hot with envy. Men of the world explored the mystery of taking off a woman's clothing and they knew the enticing touch of the silken things women wear next to their bodies. Ah, to hold a woman like Hypatia close to one's body—to feel the contours of her breasts and hips—to sense the pressure of her knees—to know the soft responsiveness of her skin! To have such a woman lying beside him, her mouth slightly open in relaxation, her body limp. . . .

Philemon turned over in bed. His body was hot and stiff with desire and his heart was pounding sharply. His eyes were wide, staring up into the blackness of his monastic room. Perhaps . . . he thought. . . . if

116

Giorgos did not come back from the Struma . . . then he would marry Hypatia and sleep next to her at night and feel her breath against his cheek, and respond to her touch during the night.

He sat up roughly to break the spell. That thought— his brother's dying—that indeed was sinful! The passion was not; he did not condemn himself for the desire of a woman's body. That was a weakness of nature, as Augustine well knew, which one could not entirely avoid. But the coveting of his brother's wife. . . . that was evil indeed!

Philemon climbed out of bed and fumbled his way in the darkness across his room to the corner where, though he could not see it, he knew the figure of Christ hung from the cross. "Christos, forgive!" he prayed. "Grant happiness and safety to my brother and his wife . . . Christos, forgive. . . ."

After his prayer he lay down again on his bed. It would indeed be pleasant, he thought, to relax like the men of the city of the world,—pleasant to love and marry and beget children. It would be a relief to give one's patriotism full reign and to fight in the ranks shoulder to shoulder with one's fellowmen, charging and dying for the beloved fatherland.

"But I have made my choice," he said to himself honestly, "and I am not sorry. It is a greater joy to aspire to the City of God, to live in the beauty which is greater than the beauty of a woman's body, and to converse with the eternal spirits of our fathers and to love the truth of God. I serve my country better here—yes, I believe it!"

And he watched the light of the moon slide through a crack in the wall, slowly cutting an arc across the floor.

*Life and Death in a Monastery*

The Australian Anzacs came up the path and stood apologetically in the opening where the big monastery door was swung agap. There were three of them. Tall and wide of shoulder, they wore broad-brimmed khaki hats at a jaunty angle. But they had a sober bearing in spite of their friendly grins. Their bronzed skin made them look like middle-aged men, though they probably were still in their twenties.

"Father," said the sergeant to Papas Demetrikos, "we have orders to set up some guns at the corner of this rock." He stepped forward, handing the abbot a paper on which a message was inscribed in Greek.

Papas Demetrikos read with a furrow in his forehead. He put the paper in his other hand, fingered his beads, and read it again. He took several steps across the cobble-stones, then back again. Then he called the Jesuit priest to explain to the Anzacs in English.

"He says, 'our buildings and our land are yours,' " the Jesuit translated. " 'Use them as our country needs. Our vows do not permit us to help you fight, but we can give you what you need.' "

The soldiers thanked Papa Demetrikos. They immediately set to work on the windlass at the corner of the monastery yard. This big wooden drum and cable was constructed on a wooden platform over the edge of the cliff. They bolstered the windlass and then let down the rusty cable which curled and dangled its way through the air. At the bottom, three hundred yards below, Philemon saw three trucks and a handful of soldiers. They seized the cable and roped it to the gun on one of the trucks. The cable strained and whined as it became taut and then wound evenly around the drum. The

118

glistening blue metal gun was hauled over the platform. Then two more were hauled up and the trucks below coughed and snorted away.

Twenty minutes later eight other Anzacs swung through the gate. They walked with a rolling motion, which kept them from showing fatigue even after a stiff climb with packs and rifles strapped to their backs. They grinned respectfully at the monks as they walked to the corner of the monastery.

Just that morning the news had come over the monastery radio that the Nazis had attacked at the Struma River. Philemon knew that Giorgos had already been stationed there. He had been called up after two days honeymoon at Volos. He was no doubt in the thick of the fight at the Struma River this very morning.

The American Jesuit hovered around the Anzacs with a strained expression, asking an occasional question, dispatching other monks in quick search of needed tools, and trying to help as best he could. The poor man's face—which two weeks earlier had shown the calm happiness of the scholar living among the books he loved— was now grimaced in continual pain. The other monks understood his conflict for they felt it themselves: it was the internal struggle between the yearning to help which swelled up with spontaneous patriotism at sight of those soldiers fighting a war which was also America's, and his conviction that as a servant of God he must not abet the war of guns and killing.

At noontime the Anzacs hoisted an Australian flag over their post and then went to relax in the cool corner of the courtyard. They opened tins of food from their packs. The Jesuit came hustling across from the kitchen carrying a tray of bean soup and eggs, almost stumbling in

his eagerness, and the soldiers accepted his gift grate-
fully.

A silence brooded over the refectory as the monks sat
at their noonday meal. Finally one of them, Michaelides, stammered in the direction of Papas Demetrikos,

"Sir, ought we—they are flying the *Anglikos* flag. Is it
not our duty to raise the flag of our own nation beside
that of our allies?"

The abbot had been staring down absent-mindedly
at a knot on the board in front of him. He lifted his
face with its wide frame of white beard.

"My son, it is right that you love your country. There
is only one thing greater than our devotion to our country. That is our love of the City of God. Never forget
the words of our father Augustine, 'The citizens of the
City of God fight with spiritual weapons—love and prayer
and truth.' "

Then Papas explained that it was fitting to hoist the
Greek flag providing the Christian flag was flown above
it. Directly after the meal Michaelides hurried to do
this. Beside the red and white stripes of the Union Jack
flew the graceful blue and white stripes of the Greek
flag, and above it, the blue cross on its white background of the Christian flag drifted in the breeze as
though it were part of the blue and white sky.

In the middle of the afternoon Philemon heard the
distant hum of airplane motors. The sound came closer,
and it puzzled him because it did not come from the
air. Then he saw three miles across the plain to the
north a rising cloud of smoke and dust.

The Anzac on duty shouted and the soldiers came
running from the courtyard.

"In hell's name," cried the sergeant, "Jerry always

120

does it—arrives ahead of schedule!" They hurriedly clicked gadgets here and there on the two larger guns, and then crouched in position, their jaws clamped in permanent smiles. Philemon stood with his back to the wall behind the windlass, watching the approaching clouds of smoke.

Three giant beetles came scurrying across the fields, the noise of their exhaust now growing into a roar. As the tanks approached the base of the fingers of rock they slowed down, nosing about in this direction and that trying to pick a way through the gap. The Anzacs squinted through their sights, steadily turning their guns as the tanks moved.

Philemon was deafened by the sudden double concussion at his side. In the cloud of smoke below he saw that both shells had hit their marks. One tank turned over on its side, the upper caterpillar tread working helplessly in the air as the steel fort cut a half circle like a skidding race-car. Another tank shivered as it recovered from the impact of the shell. It settled on its side like a truck with a broken axle. It was in the field of poppies, Philemon noticed. The black outline of the swastika was fringed with the crimson of the dense flowers. The third tank turned tail, its engines bellowing as it ran.

In the evening the Athens broadcast announced that the Nazis had broken through the Struma pass. Not one Greek had surrendered. The garrisons of the forts had died to a man. It was Thermopylae all over again.

With a loneliness that slowly began to penetrate down through his throat and into his quivering heart, Philemon realized that Giorgos had spoken truly. He would not come home from the Struma.

121

The broadcast went on to say that Larissa had been bombed unceasingly through the day. The town was a smoking ruin—not a house was left standing. Philemon felt a coldness reaching throughout his muscles. Hypatia? Had she escaped? Perhaps . . . perhaps to some peasant hut in the hills. Yes, there she could wait . . . the peasants would take care of her until this fighting was over. Oh, Christos, may it be so! She could have escaped to the hills. It's one thing for a man to die. But Hypatia! Yes, she would be safely in a little village, maybe even one of those he passed coming back on the little train. Oh God, may it be so!

But then he knew it probably was not so. There had been no warning—very few citizens could have escaped.

That night Philemon remained a long time on his knees before the figure of Christ on the cross in his room. He prayed for Giorgos. He remembered all the things Giorgaki and he used to do as children—when they made a sail for their boat and sailed all the way to Volos. And when they climbed Olympus together. And Philemon prayed for Hypatia. One can understand a man's dying as a soldier and even be proud of it—but the girl with the smile which glowed like a firefly, the girl who was frightened even of her own wedding—the thought of that body mangled gave such a cramp to his heart and stomach that he could scarcely breathe.

"O Theos, save Hypatia and Giorgos! Take them into thy heaven, O Theos. I loved them—if ever I served thee, take Hypatia and Giorgos, O Theos!"

And then he thought of the glistening guns on the corner of the cliff. Perhaps they could revenge Giorgos and Hypatia! But dare he harbor such a hope?

122

"Christos, have mercy upon us!" he prayed. "Grant strength to these men who fight to save us! Forgive us if we do not pray as we ought. We believe in thy power of truth and love, aye, we have given our lives to thee— see, thy gown, I wear it. But we are weak men, Christos, and we love our nation and our families. . . ." And here the tears that came surging up choked away his words and he clung there with his head bowed, sobbing uncontrollably on the board that served as his altar.

The next morning the tanks came back in force. Crowds of them scurried down from the north, their open exhausts roaring out their threats. A line of motorcycle troops followed discreetly on the road behind.

This time the Anzacs swung into a rhythm, a swinging of shoulders as shells were passed up, a clicking of gun chambers, punctuated by the "Hi's" and "Ready's" and the blast of anti-tank guns. The permanent smiles were still clamped on their jaws even as they swore through their teeth.

One after another of the tanks below was buried suddenly in the cloud of the exploding shells and wilted as though abruptly exhausted in its tracks. Philemon stood at the side against the framework of the windlass. Bullets spattered about the rock, hissing through the air overhead or landing with a thud in the wood. One Anzac swore and stepped back from his post with a dangling hand bleeding. The Jesuit helped him back into the monastery.

Down below, the motorcycle troops were coming up with parts of a field mortar. "Get those men on the motorcycles!" shouted the sergeant. But Philemon saw that all the Anzacs were occupied on the anti-tank guns.

He jumped forward and grabbed one of the rifles. It

would be easy enough to handle—he had often hunted with rifles in the Pindus mountains. This was an automatic, he saw. So much the better. He knelt behind a board in front of the drum of the windlass. He could rest the gun there to get a steadier sight. Three hundred yards below, the motorcycle troops were coming up to dismount.

Philemon picked out the gray figure leading the line and followed him through his gun-sights. As the motorcycle slowed down he gently increased his pressure on the trigger. With the shot, the gray figure tumbled into the ditch with his cycle on top of him.

Then the second came up, and Philemon fired again. It seemed impersonal, a job to do. He was cool in the drama which engulfed him—the noise and the rhythm of the shouting, the grinning Anzacs and his sense of being one of them.

After a quarter of an hour the motorcycle troops streaked back up the road. The tanks turned round and retired also, their exhaust bellowing off into the distance.

The Anzacs sat down and wiped their faces. "Here, man, give me a cigarette." They smoked and flexed their hands to ease stiff muscles.

"The monk here sure knows how to shoot," said one with a grin, nodding toward Philemon. Several others grunted their thanks. Though Philemon could not understand their language, he got their meaning.

"Well," said the sergeant, "Jerry will be back now with those damn dive-bombing Stukas. Get ready, men."

Philemon walked back into the courtyard in a daze. Something was wrong with this silence. His nerves were tingling, and his stomach upset. He vomited outside the monastery door. He walked dizzily to the chapel where he fell upon the floor. I killed a human being, he said to himself. After a few minutes he got up and knelt at his altar below the figure of Christ on the cross. "Christos, have mercy upon me! Forgive the sin upon my soul! Christos forgive!"

When the Stukas came half an hour later, five of them high in the air like hornets eyeing their victims, Philemon did not hear their roar.

"Christos have mercy!" he prayed. "We have broken thy law. Thou who hast suffered like us, thou who didst become a man to know our sins, and dost know our hearts. Thou too didst love a land—you taught about the lilies of the field! And thou didst love thy family and thy friends as we love ours! Take us into thy care. Ah, thou wilt forgive, Christos, blessed Christos!"

He felt himself free, free from his body as though he were lifted up by everlasting arms . . . the walls of the chapel were erased . . . he was merged with his prayer, united with Spirit . . . there was a great burst of light, and the radiance and harmony expanded to take in the whole earth and the sky . . . all was harmony and beauty and resplendence . . . he felt an ecstasy, the dizziness within him became joyful and at the same moment he was filled with a vast peacefulness. The everlasting arms held him, . . . but he needed no support . . . for all was brilliant light. He breathed the air of infinity, all about him was Being in a great exaltation . . . Was this everlasting beauty the City of God, a new city where all was peace?

Outside, the first Stuka came down like a comet, the anti-aircraft gun of the Anzacs got it. The second was already on its course, and its bomb burst directly

on the windlass, clearing that corner of the rock as though
with a broom. Philemon did not hear the explosion, for
he knelt before the altar crying out with a warm joy,
"Christos, thou dost forgive! Blessed Christos!"

The other three Stukas aimed well. Their heavy
bombs landed in the courtyard and in the row of cells.
When they soared away, the top of that finger of rock
had been blown completely clean.

# PART · III

A.M.

Detail of Greek bust, '33

# CHAPTER VII

# Paintings
## by
### THE Author

*A thing of beauty is a joy for ever:*
*Its loveliness increases; it will never*
*Pass into nothingness; but still will keep*
*A bower quiet for us, and a sleep*
*Full of sweet dreams, and health, and quiet breathing.*

JOHN KEATS

# 7

THE PICTURES THAT FOLLOW were made over a period of half a century and over two continents. They began with that historic drawing of poppies which meant so much because it was the opening of new worlds to me.

Painting is not something done chiefly with a brush and some colors. It is, rather, a way of seeing the world. I shall always remember the surprise I felt on observing the different members of a painting class working on the coast at Rockport. One would have sworn they were painting different scenes: here one emphasizes the ocean, there another makes central in his painting the two sailing vessels coming into the harbor, another sees the fishing shacks on the dock as the main theme of her painting, and so on.

You do not have to argue from the point of view of different styles—this one abstract, this one realistic, and so on. No; the important thing is that each *saw* the same world but they were painting quite distinct and different responses to this world. One's actual painting is done inside one's imagination, and it is a function of how the individual relates to the world. The threadbare story of the blind men feeling the elephant and saying it is like a rope, a piece of leather, a rug and so on, is true on a more profound level. Each of us sees the world as an individual, alone, caught up in a vast maelstrom; but by our culture we learn to communicate with our fellow human beings. Poetry, dancing, painting and other arts are all ways of communicating. The philosopher Kant said we not only see the world but the world conforms to our way of seeing it. This is certainly true in the field of art.

The great contribution of art is that, in our threescore and ten years on this planet, we are enabled to share, to give to each other, to communicate, to love the world and, in the broad sense, to love each other. This will sound strange to those who think the world is a cold mass of whirling star dust, but not to those who can form their world in communication by whatever beauty they can see and experience.

The anxiety in creating—which we see most clearly in persons like Giacometti or Michelangelo or Beethoven —is overcome by playing. As Schiller and Rank have seen, this playing (which may also be hard work) is our human way of overcoming the dualism—finite and infinite—in producing a work of art. The art unites both of these. The world becomes lonely no more, for one experiences being an integral part of it.

It used to be asked, in view of the invention and progress of photography, whether painting would not be superceded or at least made only an innocent and unnecessary pastime. The question is absurd. It rests on a radical misunderstanding of painting, the function of which is not to make a record of the external world but to share some special conception of life and the world which the painter experiences.

When I began each of these paintings, I never knew how it would turn out. One can only know that this view, this form that I see, this conception of the world, has grasped me and will not let me go until I respond. As the colors flow into each other, merging and fading, and reforming, I have a sense of participating in the universe. I experience a kind of ecstasy, great or small as it may be. And when the sketch is finished, I look at it and feel a kind of surprise, as though I had not known beforehand what I was painting. It is not that I have made something pretty or attractive; it is rather that here is a view of reality that was communicated to me, and I form it on the paper and communicate it to my friends.

The most that can be said of the following paintings is that I hope you like them, that they give you some joy, and that they tell you something about the world as I communciate with it.

PASTEL 18" X 24" PAPER, 1956

## New Hampshire Pines

When I took the children
up on a hill above Squam Lake to play
I took along my pastel crayons and pad.

*On the Beach at Nantucket*

WATERCOLOR, SUMMER, 1951

WATERCOLOR, ELMHURST, ILL. 11" x 14", SPRING, 1940

## *B lue Trees Near Chicago*

This picture shows that one can use
    almost any color that fits the design.
Marc painted blue horses,
        so why not paint blue trees.

WATERCOLOR, DEATH VALLEY, 10" x 15", 1952

## The Firey Mountain

This was the name given to the picture
by a friend who was present when I painted it.
We were both in a Volkswagen in Death Valley
with the wind howling outside.

As soon as I finished it
I immediately felt the painting was no good.
I have learned, however,
not to throw things away.
And when I looked at this a week later  I liked it.

WATERCOLOR, 6″ x 9″, DEATH VALLEY, 1970

## *After Glow of a Sunset*

This is to me the essence of watercoloring:
    it had to be done very rapidly
        (perhaps the whole thing in ten minutes)
and there is never any possibility
    of making any stroke over again
        without spoiling what has been captured.

WATERCOLOR, 11" x 14", 1984"

*View from the Island of Maui*

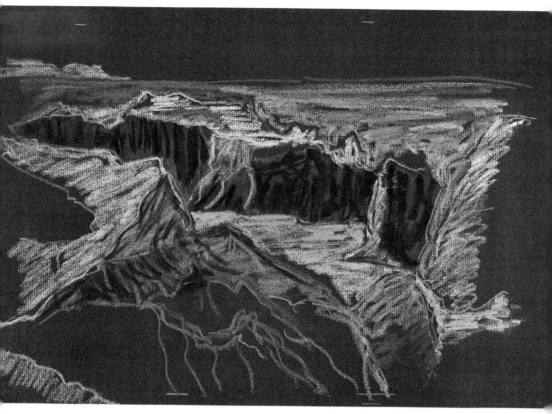

PASTELS ON BLACK PAPER, 12″ x 18″, 1980

## *Mendocino Cliffs on the Pacific Coast*

This pastel in turn seems to show the function of pastels:
to capture very quickly a fugitive moment.
It was done so early in the morning
I could scarcely see the colors on the rocks.

WATERCOLOR, 11″ x 14″, ATLANTIC

## Quiet Sea on a Lazy Noon

      I have tried many times to capture the experience
in watercolor of very soft waves lazily lapping
the sand, as though the sea were breathing.

WATERCOLOR, 11″ x 14″, BLOCK ISLAND, 1952

*The Joy of Picking Flowers*

Another excursion of the children and myself.

WATERCOLOR SKETCH, 8″ x 10″, 1980

*Three Palm Trees*    A Death Valley sketch.

WATERCOLOR, 8″ x 10″ 1952

## Nantucket

The beach seems to be a natural
for a watercolorist seeking relaxing models.

WATERCOLOR, 8½" x 11", NANTUCKET, 1952

## *C urling Pine Trees*

The rhythm of the form of these branches
is what attracted me in the woods.

# $\mathscr{A}$n Ancient Hawaiian Tree Trunk

This kind of scene aches to be painted.

WATERCOLOR, 9" x 12", 1983

*Woman
Relaxing*

WATERCOLOR, 16″ x 20″, BLOCK ISLAND, SUMMER, 1948

# *Mondays' Laundry in Rockport*

### The little Fisherman's huts are still made homes
### by artist in that picturesque town.

WATERCOLOR, 9" x 12", ROCKPORT, 1939

COLORED PENCILS, 11" x 14" PAPER, SUMMER, 1968

## Mont-St.-Michel

Scene from the Normandy Coast of France.

# CHAPTER VIII

## THE *Creative Mind*

*And if you do not find yourself beautiful yet,*
*act as the creator of a statue that is to be made beautiful:*
*he cuts away here, he smooths there,*
*he makes this line lighter, the other purer,*
*until a lovely face has grown upon his work.*
*So do you also:*
*cut away all that is excessive,*
*straighten all that is crooked,*
*bring light to all that is overcast,*
*labour to make all one glow of beauty*
*and never cease chiselling your statue,*
*until there shall shine out on you from it*
*the godlike splendor of virtue,*
*until you shall see the perfect goodness*
*surely established in the stainless shrine.*

PLOTINUS, 270 A.D.

## 8

ET US explore the human mind as it engages in the creative act. This capacity to create—which we all have, though in varying degrees—is essentially the ability to find form in chaos, to create form where there is only formlessness. This is what leads us to beauty, for beauty is that form.

Beauty reveals a form in the universe—the harmony of the spheres, as Kepler called it. It is a form which is present in the circling of the planets. It is a form which is felt in the curves and balance of our own bodies. And it is present especially in the way we see the world, for we form and reform the world in the very act of perceiving it. The imagination to do this is one of the elements that make us human beings.

Now "form" is a difficult word, partly because we derogate the term in our society. We speak of something as "merely a formality," forgetting that form is the most significant aspect of our lives. We use such depreciating phrases as "only formal" in contrast to the interesting thing called "vitality." Or we speak of "substance" rather than "empty form." These all lead to a radical misunderstanding.

On the contrary, we need to see form as the *essence*, as the very nature of the thing we are dealing with. Here Webster's Dictionary helps us: it states, *"Form is the essential nature of a thing as distinguished from the matter in which it is embodied."*

We recall Plato's ideas of the essences in heaven. These he rightly calls forms. Form is a pattern, an image and an order given to what would otherwise simply be chaos. Form is the nonmaterial structure of our lives, on the basis of which we live and on which we base our own particular character.

We recall the studies of especially creative people that were made by Frank Barron. Dr. Barron showed his cards—cards with many different drawings and paintings on them—to creative people and their counterparts, people who weren't especially creative, asking them to pick out the cards they liked best. The latter group chose the orderly cards; they liked things to be clear, understandable, uncluttered. But the creative people chose the chaotic cards. The most striking thing about the creative people was this taste for chaos. They preferred the scribbles where there was no form whatever; they found a *challenge* in the chaos. They yearned to make form out of it, "to make of the chaos about

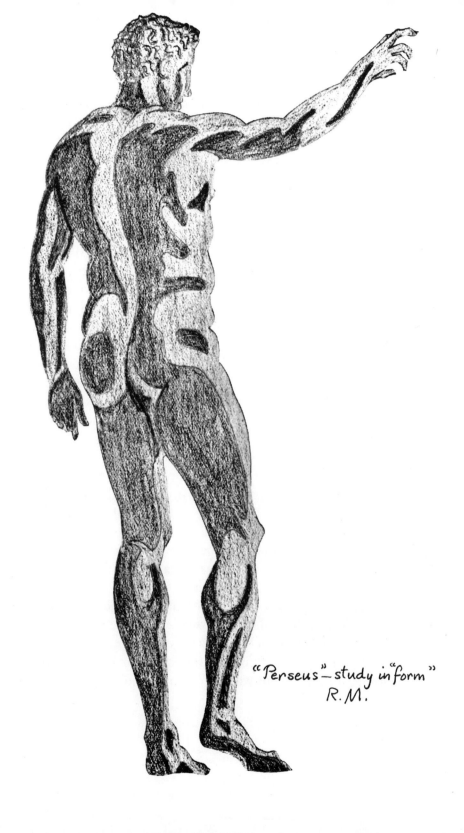

"Perseus"—study in "form"
R.M.

them an order which is their own," as Henry Miller puts it. This is the purpose of their existence. This is the fundamental *creative* aspect of all human beings whether they are especially talented or not.

The human imagination is shown in these strivings—which may sometimes be passion and sometimes simply curiosity—to put things into form. It's what Einstein did when he proclaimed that matter and energy are related in one formula, $E = mc^2$. Our human mind is continuously doing that, obviously on a lesser scale.

When I am sitting in an audience listening to a talk, I find myself making lines in my imagination from a light in the ceiling to the other lights, moving my head a little bit so that such and such will be a complete triangle, or such and such will make a perfect circle. What I happen to do it with, lines and objects, other people do with music, forming various tunes in their minds. If you are aware, I think you will find you are always subconsciously in the process of breaking something down in your imagination and putting it back together again. We do that in our ordinary reverie and we do it especially at night in our dreams. Odd things are put together—Socrates, say, is talking to the people we met yesterday. Dreams do fantastic things which seem absurd until, in thinking about the dream the next day, we find the key. All of this is a making of form.

The clearest aspect of form is obviously in architecture. The Parthenon is a dignified, majestic triumph of form. The Cathedral of Chartres is likewise magnificent form. Mont Saint Michel shows a combination of human and natural forms. The triangular form of the earth, coming up out of the water in a small mountain, is built

140

upon by human ingenuity with the triangles of Gothic architecture. One church is used as the foundation of the ones that succeeding generations erected, until finally, with the triangular peak of the last cathedral, the spire stretches up, again in triangular form, into heaven itself. We scarcely need to add that the triangle is the central symbol of medieval culture, shown not only in Gothic architecture but also in philosophy and theology in the triangle of the Father, Son and Holy Spirit.

The form dictates the content. We select, say, a sonnet to write or a drama to construct, because the content we have in mind can best be formed out of chaos and put into the particular forms of sonnet or drama or whatever form seems to fit.

There is a danger in erasing chaos too easily, for it then takes away one's stimulation. Several years ago I took the training for transcendental meditation. I have always been interested in meditating and have done it more or less on my own. When I finished that course and my mantra was given to me, I was instructed to meditate twenty minutes in the morning as soon as I woke up and twenty minutes at four or five o'clock in the afternoon. So I, being an obedient soul, started out doing that. I found that after meditating I would go down to my desk in my studio and sit there to write. And nothing would come. Everything was so peaceful, so harmonious; I was blissed out. And I had to realize through harsh experience that the secret of being a writer is to go to your desk with your mind full of chaos, full of formlessness—formlessness of the night before, formlessness which threatens you, changes you.

The essence of a writer is that out of this chaos, through struggle, or joy, or grief—through trying a dozen or perhaps a hundred ways in rewriting—one finally gets one's ideas into some kind of form. So I learned I had to meditate with discretion in the early morning in order not to lose the chaos, and to choose those times when I had finished the day's work and was ready to be blissed out with pleasure.

A drama is a drama because of its form, a ballet is a dance because of its form. Rock and roll is a rebellion against the classical form in music, and has its own form which is shown in its discords and in its special beat.

The ancient Greek philosophers set out to discover the original substance in the universe out of which all things were made. Was it air? or ether? or water? Heraclitus proposed fire. But each philosopher got trapped because the next question was, How did this element get its substance? Then came Pythagoras to cut the Gordian knot. He held that the fundamental element was no substance at all, but was really the *form* in which everything in nature is related to everything else.

Form is nonmaterial, and has its existence only as things are related to other things. When I hold up a finger on each hand, you may say that there is no relation between the two. But you would be wrong: there is the *distance* between them. If I put up another finger and draw an imaginary line among them, I would have a triangle. Or I get a cone, or a rectangle, or a circle. And soon I have an abstract drawing which is pure form!

It is not by accident that Pythagoras was the inventor not only of a great deal of mathematics (every one studies the Pythagorean theorem in geometry in high school), but also the inventor of a number of important principles in the theory of music. The tone of a violin is a vibration of a string of a certain length. Pythagoras made the famous discovery that vibrating strings under equal tension sound together in harmony if their lengths are in a simple numerical ratio. So we have laws of harmony and discord, all derivative from form. To Pythagoras is attributed the lyrical line, "The stars in the heavens sing a music if only we had the ears to hear."

Now in Pythagoras, art and mathematics were identified. This was a beautiful prediction of what was to come in our modern physics. The older concern with molecules and electrons has changed; our physicists are ready to admit that they don't really know what those are. "Something unknown is doing we don't know what," says Sir Arthur Eddington. What they do know is the relationship of one form to another; they recognize the form. They know if the form is such and such, then we have such and such a physical object.

The prototype of this significance of form is in the fascinating story of the myth of creation in the beginning of Genesis. "The earth was without form and void," it goes. This is a fantastic condition; it is the way I hope to be each morning when I go down to my studio. "And God separated the light from the darkness." Those mornings when this happens in my studio, when insights come so fast I can scarcely catch them with my pen, are great mornings!

And the myth goes on, "Then God _separated_ the sea from the land and the sky from the sea." Now separating, dividing, relating—these are all words of form. All the verbs in this fascinating myth are verbs relating to form. We read nothing about molecules or electrons, but only that God divides, separates, i.e., God *forms.*

Creativity is an emulating of God in that we destroy the cosmos and then build it up again in ways that we hope will be closer to our heart's desire. We hope and strive for the form in the rhythm which we have in our breasts, and in our heartbeat and the rhythm in our breathing.

The chaos about us is continually being reformed, only to be destroyed again by history, by nature, and by human perversity. "My photographs are a picture of the chaos in the world," remarked the artist-photographer Alfred Stieglitz, "and of my relationship to that chaos. My prints show the world's constant upsetting of man's equilibrium, and his eternal battle to reestablish it." But the works of art living on year after year are vital proof before our eyes that the reconstruction of form, of order, is eternally going on in our world. It is in this sense that the artists are the source of our conscience and our moral courage.

*Transforming One's Self*

One principle which arises in our discussion of form is the transforming of one's self which occurs in the creation of beauty. In all our creativity, we destroy and rebuild the world, and at the same time we inevitably rebuild and reform ourselves. We do this not at all in the sense of the tragedy of *The Great Gatsby,* who only changed the externals, such as his wardrobe, his accent, his bank account. We do it rather by grasping a deeper level of the form in the universe which is also in our own selves. We see the scene before us in our imagination, and that means to some extent we see our own selves. This is a very curious paradox but it is present

144

in all creative persons. "Often the creative persons in their work see the perspective of a lifetime endeavor, are themselves creating a cosmos of their own," says Frank Barron. It's as though each mind is progressively unfolding itself as one goes through life. The creative individual is the one who not only attempts to make some order out of his music or art but to make some order in his own life. A continual searching for one's forms occurs in art, and this can be automatically a search for one's own integrity.

A clear example is the life of Beethoven. He had a horrendous childhood, but his biographers relate that his creative genius was related to precisely these ordeals he suffered. His father was a drunkard, his mother died when he was young, and he had to take charge of the whole family at the age of eighteen. He never married though he passionately wanted to. But he could create such fantastic music! His biographer writes: "There is no point in Beethoven's life, where a marked development or transformation in musical styles takes place which is also not the point where an equal spiritual development occurs." That is, the spiritual development and musical style go hand in hand. The transformation of the other is also the transformation of ourselves.

Sometimes this transformation may not be good in the eyes of the artists' contemporary world. Such was the situation with Rembrandt. When he was a young man his paintings were sold on all sides; he was then what we call an outstanding success. But as he grew older and more profound, the tragic experiences in his life—the death of his children, the death of his wife— caused his paintings to take on a more somber and profound quality and made them less saleable to his fellow

Hollanders. His self-portraits reflect this: each one looks more tragic than the one before it. His popularity as a painter waned, for he would not toady to the younger generation that was coming into vogue with their glossier and more readily saleable productions. He followed undeviatingly the path of his own genius. These later creative contributions make him now recognized as the greatest painter of his age. He died in sorrow and in poverty. The people in that day considered Rembrandt a failure. We now recognize him as one of the greatest painters of all time precisely because *the transformation of himself and his art went hand and hand.*

There is another question, the relation between creativity and values. Certainly values have a great deal to do with psychotherapy, but they may seem to have very little to do with art or beauty. The studies of creative people indicate that the creative persons, so far as values go, are *amoral*, not *immoral*. They are not concerned with the generally conformist moral rules that most of us are brought up with. At the same time—and perhaps because of this freedom from conventional morality—creative persons reveal another kind of ethics. It's not rules learned by rote but rather it is *integrity itself*. It's not marriage licenses on paper but authenticity of the relationship. It's not rules of health but reverence for nature and reverence for the human body. I love the statement by Henry Miller when he says that, "the artist seeks to overthrow existing values . . . to sow strife and ferment, so that by the emotional release those who are dead may be restored to life." Then "I run with joy to the great and imperfect ones, their confusion nourishes me, their stuttering is like divine music to my ears."

As part of an art exhibit in New York, a wrecked car was dragged to the corner of a park in front of the building which housed my office. This "still life" was an entry in a show going on inside the building, but was obviously too large to drag indoors. The artists had draped a cow's intestines over the steering wheel of the car and had splashed blood over the seats. The conservative people living in the neighborhood were incensed and called the police, and in a couple of hours the wreck was hauled away. But the artists were simply trying to cry out, in as forceful a language as they could find, "This is what your technology is doing to you—take in our message!"

A great deal of modern art could be captioned under the cry, "Wake up, humanity! Be alive! Look at this world in front of you!" This is restoring the emotionally dead, resuscitating the feelingless robot, the mechanical condition into which we have been forced by adjusting to a hyper-technological civilization.

There is, on a deeper level, a very powerful relationship between beauty and ethical values. Beauty is that form in which everything is in harmony; and is that not also a definition of ethics?

A final consideration, and perhaps the most important, is that art can dispense grace. "Art," Gregory Bateson proposes, is part of "man's quest for grace." Art and the beauty which it reflects enable us to integrate ourselves. We can make a synthesis between what Freud called the "primary" and the "secondary" processes.

The function of art can also be described by the term *revelation*. Art is a constant revealing of beauty as well as truth in a sense parallel to science but in the quite different form. Art produces new knowledge, new forms, often catastrophic in its endeavor to awaken people. The revelation in art comes as an immediate and unique experience. We look at a picture and it immediately reveals a new universe, a new form of experience. This is even true of a picture we have seen hundreds of times. The Miro lithograph hanging in my living room brings me a new experience almost every time I look at it. The world is something different from what I had assumed.

There is a grace that comes in such moments; a new depth of experience in ourselves is awakened. When persons say a particular piece of music carries them into another world, they are testifying to the revelation that is in this music. Beethoven himself once remarked, "Whoever understands my music will henceforth be free of the misery of the world."

Grace comes as a gift. It is something we do not ask for and cannot command. Indeed, we do not know the new revelation even exists until it opens itself to us. We were living in a narrow world; now, with the grace that comes in art, we suddenly find ourselves in a new world we did not know was there. I recall once, on leaving an exhibit of Hans Hofmann's work, with the words singing in my mind like a Hallelujah chorus, "If a human being has the courage to paint such paintings, life surely has meaning!" It is the reverse of Dostoyevsky's sentence in the *Brothers Karamazov*, "If God is dead, everything is permitted." If such beauty exists and gives us its grace, then life must be ultimately good.

Creativity gives us a grace in the sense that it is a balm for our anxiety and a relief from our alienation. It is grace by virtue of its power to reconcile us to our

148

deepest selves, to lead us to our own depths where primary and secondary functions are unified. Here the right brain and the left brain work together in seeing the wholeness of our world.

And thus my painting and the creative sketching—indeed, _everyone's_ creative acts, whatever they may be—make constructive form out of the apparent formlessness of our lives.

# CHAPTER IX

## Art & Symbols

*Symbolism is no mere idle fancy
or corrupt degeneration:
it is inherent
in the very texture of human life. . . .
Mankind, it seems,
has to find a symbol
in order to express itself.*

ALFRED NORTH WHITEHEAD

## 9

W HEN PICASSO paints a portrait of Gertrude Stein with one large eye in the middle of her forehead, what is he trying to communicate? When Cézanne gives this advice to young painters, "Paint nature in cubes, rectangles and planes," what is he saying? Gertrude Stein has two eyes like the rest of us; Cézanne knows that there is no pure cube or rectangle in nature.

Picasso and Cézanne are speaking in symbols.

*What are Symbols?*

A symbol is a condensed way of saying something below our customary discursive language. For that reason, symbols speak on several levels at once. A stop sign at the corner says only one thing, namely stop at that corner, and is understood by everyone from three years of age on. But a symbol is an image, a form which communicates many things at once. This gives the symbol its rich meaning and its power to delight us.

Picasso is saying that he sees in Gertrude Stein a strong woman with commanding manner; she looks at you with the power of an X-ray machine. Cezanne sees nature as much more than simple trees and clouds. He sees symbols which take in all the vertical lines in the world from a yardstick to a laser beam, and cones in all the curving lines of mountains and shores, say of Mont Saint Victoire and its lake, which he painted many times. He wants the young painters to grasp nature not superficially but in its heart and soul.

"A symbol, indeed, assumes two planes," writes Albert Camus, "two worlds of ideas and sensations, and a dictionary of correspondences between them. This lexicon is the hardest thing of all to draw up. But awakening to the two worlds brought face to face is tantamount to getting on the trail of their secret relationships."

It may help us to get on this "trail" of symbols in art if I recount an experience of my own on a ship in the Mediterranean. I stood on the prow of a Greek ship steaming into the harbor of Istanbul. I saw the flags of the different nations flying from the masts of the vessels in the harbor. I noticed the red and black of the Turkish flag, the yellow and red of the Rumanian and the French tricolor. I observed these colored cloths with interest, noted the various nations to which they belonged, and mused on how many countries it takes to make up Europe.

Then, as my ship passed round the bend of the Golden Horn, I suddenly saw an American flag. My reaction

154

was entirely different. I had an experience that grasped my total self—a surging moment of joy, then a longing for my country which I had not seen for two years. My mind was flooded with all the rich and potent connotations of homeland. I recalled my childhood in Michigan, and I felt a surge of loneliness for my parents and brothers and sisters who were still back there. The sight of the flag also cued off my conflicts about being American and identified with that country: I felt a guilt similar to what I felt during our recent Vietnam tragedy. I felt again the moral conflict and the daimonic sense of nationalistic power.

The flags of other countries were signs. The flag of my own country was a symbol.

Artistic symbols and myths speak out of the primordial, preconscious realm of the mind which is powerful and chaotic. Both symbol and myth are ways of bringing order and form into this chaos. Mark Schorer describes symbols and myths well when he calls them "instruments by which we continually struggle to make our experience intelligible to ourselves." Myth is a large controlling image which gives meaning to the ordinary facts of life, and symbol is a small image which performs a similar function for specific events. Both are our ways of organizing our experience so that it makes sense.

Dreams are so valuable because they are made up of symbols. One of my patients, who had been an actress, had the following dream. Her forehead had been cut and was bleeding. She didn't know what to do to stop the flow of blood. She then realized in the dream that she could put a kotex on it, which, she said to me, "was alright if you didn't mind."

Here we have this simple symbol of the cut forehead

and the kotex. As we analyzed it, we arrived first at the meaning that she was hurt and needed my services as a psychotherapist. Then we go deeper and find that the symbol shows a "positive transference," i.e., she had fantasies of wanting to have sexual intercourse with me, the therapist, but she is ambivalent about it: the kotex is not used to prepare for intercourse but to cover the vagina during menstruation. This woman had been very unfeeling so far as sex with men was concerned; she thought—it turned out mistakenly—that she was lesbian. But the wound was in her head, the organ of thinking, rationality. Thus the symbols say that one of her problems was intellectualizing—which indeed was true.

But there is still another meaning to the symbol in this woman's case-history, which takes us far back into mythology. This is the ancient myth of Athena's birth: Zeus was cloven in the forehead and out lept Athena from his head, an adult fully armed. This opens up a whole vista of new meanings. First, she makes me Zeus, the chief of the gods on Mt. Olympus. And second, she makes herself Athena, a fully armed woman (Athena makes a good pattern for a lesbian since she did not love a male nor ever experience sexuality). Athena had great power, intelligence and notoriety; she was the goddess of Athens, the city which was named after her. It is "my city," she calls it in Aeschylus, and she does all these wonderful things which turn it into a great Mecca of civilization.

So! My patient produces a brilliant, revealing and confident image of herself, despite her problems.

One can pursue almost every symbol to such great lengths. We could say in therapy that one symbol used by a person in a dream has within it the person's whole life. Hence symbols are so important in psychotherapy and art—and in all of life.

### Symbols and Evil

Immediately we find ourselves asking about the ethical implications of art as it uses various symbols. It is important to remember that symbols are "beyond good and evil" in their first blush of birth. It is only later that reason rightly undertakes to distinguish the constructive and destructive elements in a given symbol or myth.

The word "symbol" comes from two Greek words *syn* and *ballein* meaning "to draw together." The antonym of "symbolic"—a fact overlooked by most people—is "diabolic." This word comes from the Greek *dia* plus *ballein*, and means to "tear apart, to confuse, to throw into discord." In the Genesis story of creation, the devil functions in exactly this way: he divides, sows discord between "Adam" and "Eve," and between them and God. We may recall, too, Hitler's diabolic use of symbols—the swastika, for example—in the service of racism and genocide.

This brief excursion into etymology implies a whole system of ethics. The *good* is that which makes for understanding, communication, communion. This is certainly true in relations between nations, and is as true if more ambiguous in intrapsychic and interpsychic relationships. From Kierkegaard to Harry Stack Sullivan among the moderns, it has been emphasized that psychological ill-health is due to a radical inability to communicate with one's world, and that psychological integration is the capacity to establish enduring interpersonal relationships.

All of us have experienced the profound relief and the genuine catharsis when we get our resentment "off our chest." William Blake's famous verse is as true as it ever was:

> I was angry with my friend:
> I told my wrath, my wrath did end.
> I was angry with my foe;
> I told it not, my wrath did grow.

As if to fit exactly into our discussion, Blake goes into mythology to clinch his point in the last verse:

> And it grew both day and night,
> Till it bore an apple bright;
> And my foe beheld it shine,
> And he knew that it was mine.

How enthralling is that artistic symbol of the "apple!"—the apple as in the Garden of Eden. Blake is saying that anger feeds upon itself; and one experiences the double punishment of personal humiliation in one's foe being able to see "that it was mine."

Evil, in this system of ethics, is that which tears apart, shuts out the other person, raises barriers, sets people against each other. Speaking intrapsychically, the individual is locked up with himself alone. Like the damming of a river, his vitality backs up and becomes brackish and unhealthy and a breeding ground for germs. He is shut up *from* his life, not, as Kierkegaard puts it in contrast, shut up *with* something—which latter may instead be constructive solitude. Diabolism refers to evil inherent in the process of being torn apart, the spreading of calumny.

Thus Hitler had to have a scapegoat to keep his regime going, had to have war as a necessary means of gaining unity among the German people by setting them against the rest of the world. Hitler was a man with both a daimonic and a diabolic imagination. Strangely, he was so often right. He chose symbols which were directly linked to people's deepest hopes and fears. I hate all that Hitler stood for, but one can deal with symbols best by not running away from them. If his symbols were to work, Hitler had to pick some group to be the scapegoats, for which he chose the Jews. That was the diabolic side of his symbolic imagination. The symbols he chose were shrewd, effective, tremendously powerful. With them he squeezed a tremendous war out of the German Army. Risenthal in his propaganda films used Hitler's symbols effectively: you see the swastika, you hear the Wagnerian music, you see the marching armies and you see this charismatic leader speaking in his high-pitched, strong German.

Symbols and myths are neither ethical nor demonic in themselves: it's how they're used that makes the difference. Hitler couldn't have been changed by rational or logical arguments. Our government could not understand this. We in this country were rationalistic people and we didn't allow what was happening to get inside our feelings—therefore we couldn't conceive of what Hitler was up to. If we realize that people can be devilish, we can be better prepared to deal with them.

Hitler's intense attacks on modern art should have tipped us off, since artists cannot help telling the truth. They are our early-warning mechanism. The German artists like George Grosz and Max Beckmann satirized the German mood in the early '30's, painting fat

armament builders smoking expensive cigars and
watching a flapper floor show. Hitler called this deca-
dent art, and held up the art world to ridicule. The
lower middle class in Germany went to the galleries to
mock modern art. This was another early-warning
mechanism which we in the United States ignored.

But a country's or leader's symbols obviously don't
have to be diabolic, as Hitler's were. The example of
my experience of the symbol of the American flag in
Istanbul illustrates two things. The other nations' flags
were *signs;* they stood *for* something, and I decoded and
filed them away in my mind as discrete facts. But the
flag of my own country grasped me as a total being,
even to the point of my loneliness, my pride and guilt
feeling. Thus a symbol does not stand *for* something,
but it is a symbol *of* something. A sign can be *intellec-
tualized.* But symbols can be apprehended only as *images,* and are most effective when taken thus, as artists
do.

The symbol of the American flag illustrates, in our
post-Vietnam day, how a symbol becomes ambiguous
and then goes through a process of metamorphosis.
Multitudes of citizens in this day of post-Vietnam, and
of Watergate and of similar crises, which they interpret
as black marks on the escutcheon of the United States,
have expressed their moral indignation at the flag, this
symbol of their country.

Do we achieve anything by degrading the symbol, or
by burning the flag? What is changed by putting it to
utilitarian use, i.e., wearing clothes made from the flag?
How does spitting on the flag show contempt for a national policy? In asking these questions, we are already
assuming the symbol *is* the nation in some strange way.

Many of us, trying to bring reason to bear on the evolution of a symbol, ask ourselves: Can the meaning of the flag be enlarged to symbolize the internationalism that we see as part of the wave of the future? Can the flag be stretched to encompass planetism? Can the loyalty it supposedly engenders be stretched to include other nations? How can we achieve a viable flag of the United Nations, or of NATO? I cite these questions as illustrating the process of metamorphosis through which every living art and symbol must go as we move into a new world.

### Symbols and the Artist

In the times of the creation of symbols, the function of the artist is to _create new order_. In times of excessively rigid symbols, in contrast, the function of the artist is to _create chaos_. This latter is the challenge facing modern artists. The artists are concerned with form and the breaking up of misused form. This is so not only of the professional artist but of the artist in each of us. The German poet Hölderlin wrote that when danger increases, the power to meet it also increases. Hölderlin was a great poet and a schizophrenic at the same time; his pathology was related to his poetic talent. Thus epilepsy was called in ancient times the god-given illness, and it was thought by some persons in ancient Greece that psychosis produced poetry and profound inspiration. That's why great art often emerges in the aftermath of a breakdown. Some of the new artistic sensibility may reside in those very pathological aspects of life.

In light of this, I think it would be very important if we would value our breakdowns more, take more

interest in our so-called neurotic symbols. Our breakdowns are often the place where we discover our voca-
tions as artists or other professionals. And pathological
tendencies often reveal and enrich the artist's repertoire
of symbols.

I've been very grateful for that so-called breakdown
back when I was twenty-one, which I referred to at the
beginning of this book. That event forced me to "wake
up" to life, to feel, not to go through life somnambul-
istically, not to let my neurotic patterns block off my
appreciation of beauty. If it hadn't been for my inner
chaos, I probably would have thought, "Well, these fields
of red poppies are pretty," and gone on to ignore them.
As it was, I felt a kinship with them in my loneliness;
I picked a poppy and studied it tenderly. I felt a kinship with the whole of nature, with the universe of dawns
and stars; I had been jarred out of my old routine. In
this respect a "breakdown"—i.e., when you strike a
psychological road block—can be a very valuable experience. The times when you are wounded are often times
when, out of these wounds, come new thoughts, new
possibilities. Art and the beauty from which it comes
make us stop and take inventory of our lives.

Art and its symbols disrupt and enrich us who receive
them, whether they are "pretty" or not. The richness
of the artistic symbol is a richness of you and me, the
receivers. The viewer thinks and feels a symbol, and
by that symbol he gets his artistic response. For example, I am walking along a street and I see a cross in a
shop window. I pay no attention to it at first, but four
or five steps down the street I suddenly get a lot of
ideas. Perhaps it symbolizes the crucifixion? Or perhaps
it is a Ku Klux Klan cross, to be burned in that yard

across the street? Or perhaps it is an advertisement for the Red Cross. Thus the symbol cues off in me, the viewer, the agony of the Ku Klux Klan's cross or the ideal meaning of the Christian cross, as well as other possible meanings. Those responses are obviously not in the symbol itself; they're in us, the viewers. But you can't feel them until the symbol hits you. You cannot think in that rich way except with the help of symbols.

Eric Kahler points out that a symbol is a bridging act. It puts together rational *and* emotional, cognitive *and* conative, past *and* present, individual *and* social, conscious *and* unconscious. All these are formed together as a montage. Marshall McLuhan, similarly, uses the figure of transparency: a symbol is a collage of transparent items. You can see through the top one to the various levels below and behind it, which is one way to look at Rothko's and Olitski's paintings.

*To Disguise and to Reveal*

A symbol's function is to cover up and to reveal, to disguise and to disclose simultaneously. The connotation of the term *symbolic* is precisely this artistic capacity to disguise and at the same moment to disclose, one being impossible without the other. A symbol in a dream covers up an immediate reality and at the same time discloses a deeper reality.

A young woman dreamt of a black buoy in the water as a symbol of the phallus of her black sweetheart. This is, first, obviously a *disguise* for what she is concerned with, namely sex with a partner of which her family disapproves. She laughed at the picturesque nature of the symbol, since bouys in her lake were longish poles that stuck up out of the water. But at the same time this symbol also reveals a good deal more. The essence of a buoy is that it gives security; one can tie one's boat to it in the midst of all the tumultuous waves of life, secure in a lake or ocean. She may need the security to support her in her struggle against her own mother. All these pointers immediately begin the process of disclosure. The revelation is as much the function of the symbol as the disguising. It is only through the revelations which the symbol brings into consciousness that we are able to understand the meaning for a given person's defenses, strategies and other tensions in psychotherapy.

The use of symbols in art is a way of grasping and communicating reality directly and immediately. We don't need a long speech to understand Gertrude Stein's power of "staring into" whomever she looks at; we need only look at Picasso's painting of her. The symbol unites past and present, conscious and unconscious, individual and social. All these were present in my seeing the American flag from my ship in Istanbul in contrast to other flags. The genius of the symbol in art is that it brings together all these levels of life that rationally are separated. We use symbols to unite these diverse elements in our own experience.

We speak of art as "symbol and myth," for they are both means by which we perceive life; they are the frames through which we make sense of the kaleidoscopic activity about us and in us. The symbol and myth are not ways of getting *a* perspective; they are *the perspective itself*. No one would argue that we do not *project* the symbol and myth; we do. But no one ought also to protest against the equally obvious fact that the objective world is present in the symbol and myth as the stimulus, the setting of the problems we seek to resolve, the data we try to assimilate and make meaningful. Hence, art, like all expressions of beauty, is subjective and objective at the same time.

The symbol *participates in the thing it symbolizes*. The Christian cross is in actuality simply two sticks of wood placed at right angles to each other. But symbolically its form means infinitely more. The cross is the vertical dimension crossing the horizontal; the spiritual and the worldly levels crossing each other, engaged in perpetual tension and hopefully producing creative religious ideas and actions as an expression of this tension.

Take the symbol of water at St. Anne des Pres, in Quebec, the Canadian shrine of healing waters like Lourdes. The priests at St. Anne have placed signs at various places where the water springs out of the ground, explaining that it is the faith in God which heals you, of which the water is a symbol. But water is also a healing agent and has been one since time immemorial; it has cleansing, health-giving properties. Water participates in the healing process though it is God who performs the cure. Also, signs point out that you may be "cured" psychologically and spiritually without being "cured" physically. One can see the struggle the theologians have had to preserve the shrine from magic, and they do this by emphasizing the faith in God, with the water as a curative agent which is the symbol of the activity of God. He produces healing waters, symbolic and diabolic, just as he did at the time of Noah and the flood.

The symbol *points beyond itself*. "A symbol always transcends the one who makes use of it and makes him say in reality more than he is aware of expressing," writes

Camus. This is partly because of the multitude of dimensions the symbol encompasses; one cannot help expressing more than he is conscious of. This is part of the functioning of the double symbolic dimension of art as revealing and disclosing. The reason for the prejudice against, or perhaps more accurately, the *fear* of, symbols and myths in art is that they disclose so much; thus I cannot know exactly what I'm saying. I have a tiger by the tail, and I rightly fear being carried by this animal faster and farther than I want to go.

This reminds me of a cartoon in *The New Yorker*. A society woman is taking a revolver out of her handbag as she gets up from the analyst's couch. She is saying, "This has been very nice, Doctor, but you know too much."

Art releases and stimulates imagination among others to whom you are talking as well as yourself. How much easier to remain pedestrian, walking only along well-known city blocks of rational, completely circumspect expression! This anxiety is seen often in people in psychoanalysis: they guard what they tell the analyst, or tell only the dreams they've been able to fumigate by discussing with a friend or spouse beforehand lest they tell the analyst more than they themselves can understand. This is obviously a futile procedure: if you wish to make progress in creating or participating in psychotherapy, you've got to risk revealing all kinds of "dangerous" things. For no symbols or myths can be harnessed to merely a conscious meaning. "All that happens is symbol," said Goethe, "and as it represents itself perfectly, it points to the rest."

Through its symbols, art is energy-releasing. Drawing together into a meaningful circle the many data flooding in on us, the artistic symbol frees us from confusion; we are not continually overwhelmed by the kaleidoscopic bombardment of experience. One can either block off the experience—which is the solution on the side of apathy, self-protection, death; or one can organize these multitudinous events into meanings that can then be dealt with as symbols—which our capacity of symbol-forming enables us to do.

The symbol also draws out our need to will and to act. This is part of its function in making experience meaningful. Once we are freed from the unbearable confusion, we see our experience in manageable forms; and we do exactly that, we *manage* it, we take some stand with respect to it. For many Jews, Hanukkah is the symbol not only of eternal light but of pogroms, painful experiences of relatives who suffered in many countries, personal struggles, hope and new possibilities. For the believing Jew all these things not only are exceedingly meaningful but they require of the Jew some stand, which may be renewed consecration or resoluteness. One cannot let one's self be grasped fully by a symbol without experiencing the feeling that a change in one's life is necessary.

Thus the symbol gives wings to the imagination. It casts one loose as the young eagle is cast out of the nest. The function of the myth and symbol is seen in the writings of James Joyce like *Ulysses:* the different tenses are represented simultaneously; fantasy and actuality are mixed, as they are in immediate existence anyway. Each sentence comes across like a chord on the piano: notes of a number of different pitches are encompassed into one harmony.

*Films as Art and Symbol*

The genius of the films as an art form is that they can re-enact myth and symbol. In films we can combine fantasy and actuality, unite past and present and future; and what the beholder sees is not merely a spectacle. He experiences in his own emotions what the character on the screen is experiencing. As was demonstrated so well in the Italian film "8-½," you experience this "hero" through his fantasies, his daydreams, his anxieties and hopes and fears, his plans and his memories. In this sense movies have claim to being the unique art form for our day. They can move instantaneously from childhood, to the present, to an imagined future, and can move from action to fantasy at will. Their genius is in encompassing and stimulating the imagination of the viewer.

This is why hard-core pornographic films so often lose their own power as well as the power of the genre. By being too literal in their sexual production they stifle the imagination rather than giving it wings. One's fantasy is made impossible by the concreteness of the image; the fantasy, which is the symbolic and mythic character, is lost because the viewer is forced to be only a spectator—he or she cannot participate in the process of the movie itself. The mystery which infuses sexuality and sexual love, which is necessary in order to grasp the deeper aspects of the experience in one's imagination, becomes destroyed; and you have a ridiculous picture of two people nakedly cavorting on the screen. This achieves its attraction out of the power of rebellion against the Establishment, but it has nothing to do with the film as art, and the effect will be temporary in any case. The *art* of films can become *artifice* easily enough and, surrendering its birthright, it can become a mere

168

spectacle to be judged by the dollars-and-cents yardstick of the marketplace.

How different is the bas-relief of Leda and the Swan.
This is not pornographic at all, though the image might
be misinterpreted that way in our day. It is a beautiful
carving, harmoniously bringing these two forms into the
square, each line becoming part of a totality which is
woven together with the serenity we expect from great
Greek art. The joy it gives has nothing to do with sex;
it is the joy that goes with the serenity of beauty.

Film and sculpture are examples of ways symbol and
myth help us manage the problem of time by confronting it and taking it into our total scheme of life. Most
of us are afraid of time. The fear of time—the inexora-
ble rolling on of fate, of entropy in our universe which
continues even though we may blot out our awareness
of it by drugs or alcohol—is paralleled by our bodies
growing old. It is a threat indeed, and a source of our
most severe anxiety. The experience of time hanging
heavy over our heads like a sword of Damocles is a subjective phenomenon, private and personal. The symbol
and the myth are our ways of holding its threats at bay.
The many myths of afterlife—heaven, reincarnation, the
"final conflict" of the Marxists—are examples. The myth
of progress and the myths of what Lifton calls "symbolic immortality," are all parts of our struggle to make
time meaningful.

*Symbols and Civilization*

Symbols, finally, are our source of freedom and civilization. That is, from our capacity to form into symbols
the mass of experiences which impinge upon us as in-
fants, we are able to establish some distance from the

169

world in which we can infuse meaning into our experience.

The symbol-forming process is not born with the birth
of the infant but begins to emerge after ten or twelve
months. It is one aspect of the development of the infant's capacity for self-consciousness. This growth is required before the infant is mature enough to abstract
itself from the situation and to embrace itself and the
world in the same concept. Between these two opposite
things—self on the one hand and world on the other—
there is a greater or lesser tension. We call this tension
"awakeness," "alertness."

It is out of this tension that symbols are born. Symbols, and symbolic thinking, are one aspect of consciousness and self-awareness. The capacity to be aware
that I am telling the truth emerges simultaneously with
my capacity for telling a lie, as Jean-Paul Sartre tells us
in his statement, "the lie is a behavior of transcendence."

When, say, from the first to the third year, the symbols the infant picks up are too rigid and dogmatic, made
so by too much anxiety on the infant's part arising from
over-permissiveness or over-rigidity on the part of the
parents, the infant's capacity to develop symbols is par-
tially blocked. A rigidity is begun which limits not only
the child's symbol-forming from then on, but also the
child's openness to the countless symbols that are available in our culture. Then we have a rigid, unfree, driven
person, who in later life may well be termed neurotic.
This is the curtailing and destruction in the person of
the capacity to grow, to change, to create. It may set an
almost insurmountable barrier for the creativity of art
later on, or the child, when he gets to be adult, may

well revolt against the whole society and become an artist!

Just as the symbol-forming power may be arrested in individuals, so also it may be altered, for good or ill, in whole populations. For civilizations are themselves dependent precisely on symbolism. "By superseding instinct, the symbol makes civilization possible," the philosopher Alfred North Whitehead wrote. He was aware that symbolism is so woven into our civilization that our language depends on it. "The world is a symbol, and its meaning is constituted by the ideas, images and emotions, which it raises in the mind of the hearer." Language, art and symbolism on the deeper level are identical.

For symbolism is our stand against the rule of sheer instinct. It is the bulwark by which civilization and art tame sheer instinct. "In place of the force of instinct which suppresses individuality, society has gained the efficacy of symbols, at once preservative of the commonweal and the individual standpoint," says Whitehead.

The function of reason, Whitehead emphasizes, is not at all to compete with symbols or to try to suppress all symbols and myths. It is to judge between them. Reason should rightly operate to purify and clarify symbols; it is suicidal to try by reason to destroy them.

Advances in civilization threaten the very society which discovers them, writes Whitehead, in his study _Symbolism in Religion and Literature:_

> The art of free society consists first in the maintenance of a symbolic code; and secondly in the fearlessness of revision, to secure that the code

serves those purposes which satisfy an enlightened
reason. Those societies which cannot combine reverence to their symbols with freedom of revision,
must ultimately decay either from anarchy, or from
the slow atrophy of life stifled by useless shadows.

Artists know this intuitively. With fearless energy,
poets, painters, musicians and sculptors expose us to
the contents of the symbols. Often the results of such
creative action disconcert us. But the artist's job is not
to comfort—nor even to inform and instruct.

The artist's purpose is to liberate, to cleanse the creative process of those rationalized accretions which we
invent in order to shield ourselves from the powerful
truth of authentic symbols. Good art wounds as well as
delights. It must, because our defenses against the truth
are wound so tightly around us. But as art chips away
at our defenses, it also opens us to healing potentialities
that transcend intellectual games and ego-preserving
strategies.

The future of our civilization, its survival and health,
is inseparable from the future of its art. Modern art is
thus neither a luxury nor a decorative excrescence
hanging on the edges of culture. Art is central to any
civilization which hopes to remain vital and healthy.

# PART · IV

Leda and the Swan, bas relief
in the National Museum, Athens,
drawn in 1933.

# CHAPTER X

# Myth
## AS AN Art Form

*Art is contemplation. . . .*
*It is the joy of intelligence.*

AUGUSTE RODIN

# *10*

MYTH IS a narration which assumes an art form and thus becomes universalized. Myth has the symbolic power of art, and like any work of art, myths help us to make sense of our world. Like other forms of art, myths relieve our excessive anxiety and guilt feeling and enable us to live in times of turmoil with some inner balance and peace. Myth enables us to experience the universal meaning—say of love, of death, of joy, and even of adversity.

More specifically, myth as an art form enables us to confront the events that would be the most hideous, such as the crucifixion of Christ, and to make of that hideousness a form of beauty and meaning. The Son of Man and the Son of God lives out the grand scenario of the suffering servant and then dies that all of us may be saved. How powerful this scenario is! It makes one understand (though not necessarily agree with) the fundamentalist ministers who say "We preach Christ crucified and risen from the dead."

Consider how many thousands of paintings have been made of the crucifixion through western history, from Cimabue's through El Greco's to the most insignificant canvas in the Vatican. This myth has inspired almost every painter in Christendom to give his version of the heroic happening. And consider how many statues have universalized Christ's suffering, from the countless mosaics to Michelangelo's "Pietà" down to the crucifixes on the walls of hundreds of thousands of churches. The great beauty that such a cruel scene calls forth is astonishing indeed.

The same is true of that most hideous of all events in our recent history, the Vietnam War. This war threw into focus one gruesome happening after another—like Calley's massacre of the women, children and old people in the helpless Vietnamese village of My Lai, or President Johnson's lying to us as the Pentagon papers showed. How do we heal such wounds to our minds? We can try to forget, but that would be cruel and it never works anyway.

But the myths do exercise a healing balm, as shown in that very mythic film, *Apocalypse Now*. Call to mind the scene at night where the Marine is firing shells off into the maelstrom of bursting bombs that makes a ghastly day out of the blackness. When the interlocutor asks him where his commander is, the marine shouts above the uproar of the exploding shells that he doesn't know where his commander is, or what his name is, or whether he even *has* any commander; he only hastens to keep shooting his shells into the bursting sky. What more graphic picture of the gross irrationality of modern warfare! This universalizes the experience; we can see it in the perspective of all man's cruelty to man.

The whole film can be viewed, as fortunately most people did view it, not as violence at all but as the choreography of warfare. Each actor dances out his or her role, from the shots of the helicopters raiding the village to the tune of Wagner's *Ride of the Valkyries,* to the dance of the sexy entertainers mobbed by thousands of sex-starved soldiers, to the final scene of the ruler of the jungle encampment being beaten to death with a baseball bat and mumbling as he dies, "Horror, horror." What more powerful way could there be to portray the sheer ghastly horror of contemporary warfare?

Seeing the film as mythic, we are freed from excessive anxiety in strange ways. We see the war in perspective; we see it externalized, made universal. We conceive of the war as part of the long path down through the ages of man's inhumanity to man. This relieves us of excessive guilt: it is not just ourselves who cause this choreography of horror; war is a human paradox. But this is in no sense an escape from responsibility, for we are then better able to act, to protest, to prevent this happening again. We do not wish to "forget Vietnam," as President Ford adjured us to do—that would only add neurosis to evil, and lead us sooner into other such "horrors." But we are able to see it with less personal self-punishment and greater resolve to work toward compassion in our international relationships.

This property of myth is rightly called "externalization" by Jerome Bruner. This means that myth places an inner perception, say of our feelings of horror of the

Vietnam War, outside us in the symbolism of this film. Thus that myth overcomes the split between what is subjective and what is objective, the split between irrational and rational. Bruner cites from the *Iliad* an interesting demonstration of this, the story of Achilles's armor. When Achilles is slain, his mother, Thetis, a river nymph, ruled that her son's armor should go to the bravest of the Greeks. Agamemnon must make the fateful decision. He rules that Odysseus shall have the arms. This enrages Ajax, who had considered himself the bravest, and in his passion for vengeance he sets out to slay his fellow Achaeans. But at this crucial spot the myth steps in—Athena intervenes. She strikes Ajax mad so that he goes about slaughtering the captured cattle of the Trojans, cursing Agamemnon and Odysseus and Menelaus as he does it. The rage is turned, by way of the myth, away from the actual deed which would have decimated the whole Greek army. In our present psychological language we would call this, as Bruner does, a massive displacement of aggression. The myth then saves the whole Trojan project from being destroyed by Ajax. The myth as an art form dilutes the irrationality, in this case of Ajax's rage, and turns it into a relatively harmless form, namely, slaughtering the Trojan cattle.

Far from being irrational, myths actually save us from irrationality. They make our powerful emotions, which would drive us into psychosis otherwise, into diluted forms which we can absorb. And they do that by virtue of being an art form, as the *Iliad* and *Apocalypse Now* are art forms.

The myth has certain characteristics which it shares with other art forms, like poetry, the novel, painting, sculpture, music and dance. These shared characteristics include harmony, balance, rhythm. They are qualities which minister to our inner needs for serenity, for a sense of eternity, and ultimately for courage. All genuine works of art give a sense of meaning which informs us that life is more significant than the disasters, petty or great, which clamor for our attention. "Music hath charms to soothe the savage breast" is attested by numberless events through history like King Saul calling upon David to play music to soothe his madness. The Greeks seem to have been particularly aware of these forms of beauty, and they were not hampered by any commandment against making graven images, as the Hebrews were in their Ten Commandments.

We have said that the beauty which myths bring to us is a source of their healing power. Within the explosion into their wonderful civilization, the ancient Greeks had a devotion to beauty that was singularly great. One has only to walk through the National Museum at Athens, or the room containing the Elgin marbles in the British Museum in London, to see, in the sheer number of statues, what great heights and depths this civilization produced. This is surely related to the Greeks' vast fecundity for myths.

This causes us to pause over the most notorious myth of all, and one often neglected in favor of the less known dramas, the myth of Helen of Troy. On reading the *Iliad*, most people would take Helen to be a faithless, superficial hussy, and they would regard it a miscalculation of great proportions that Menelaus and Agamemnon, Achilles and Ulysses, and all the other famous heroes in the Greek hosts should have journeyed over the sea to Troy to fight for ten years, losing many a noble warrior in the war, just to bring back this woman. If one is in modern Greece, one hears from citizens such theories as that the war was really fought over sailing routes and the wheat that was transported through the Hellespont, and so on. But such theories grossly underestimate the versatility of the ancient Greeks. We have not asked the obvious question underlying this journey, that is, for what function in human experience was the myth of Helen?

I propose the simplest and most direct answer to that question: *Helen is the myth of beauty.* There is an interesting episode in the *Iliad*, when Homer pictures two Trojan soldiers on the city walls in the cold of night around a little fire they have built to keep warm. They are bewailing the war, and how pointless it was from the start. Then Helen suddenly comes out of her house and the men watch her as she walks along the ramparts. They change completely; one proclaims, "This war must go on!," and their spirits are rededicated to the war.

What is the meaning of this? Certainly not sex appeal, or her attractiveness as a fashion queen. Indeed, in the bas-relief of Leda and the Swan, the myth of Zeus camouflaged as a swan and having intercourse with the lovely Leda shows clearly the difference between beauty and pornography or sex appeal. In this charming form there is no pornography whatever. The figures show the beauty of perfect balance, curved lines that meet and repeat each other like a piece of music, a union of the form of Leda's body meeting the form of the Swan. The whole picture has a sense of eternity, the union of human and divine, in a calmness that impressed me fifty years ago and impresses me even more today.

Especially in the myth of Helen of Troy is it necessary to distinguish between pornography and genuine beauty, a distinction made not only by classical Greece but also by our modern writer, James Joyce. This contemporary author held that when an actor or actress, or writer for that matter, tries to elicit a specific emotion, such as mirth or grief or fear or sexuality, the result is not beauty but pornography. Beauty, holds Joyce in agreement with the ancient Greeks, shows a state of being as ontological, rather than as an emotion which can be turned on or off. This saves us from confusing movie actresses, or Miss Americas, or various attractive bodies advertising bikinis, with actual beauty. Some actors and actresses have some beauty, there is no doubt— Ingrid Bergman and Greta Garbo, for example. But it is in spite of the sex appeal rather than because of it. because of it.

I propose that Helen of Troy was the symbol for Beauty Itself. For beauty was the condition of harmony between different truths and different deeds of virtue; and in this sense it was the aspect of *Arētē* that needed most to be cultivated, the treasure of all human aspiration.

This could well be the secret of the greatness of Greece, above all the arguments concerning the power given by their enthusiasm at driving back the Persians in 490 and 480 B.C., or all the explanations on the basis of the riches of Athens in this fifth century with its slave populations, and all the other contemporary arguments of our sociologists and psychologists. We are pushed back to the simplest explanation of all: that Helen was the symbol of Beauty and the myth meant just what it said, namely, that Beauty was worth the whole expedition to Troy. We capitalize the term because the word now takes on divinity for the Greeks: Helen is later made a goddess. It may thus be that the greatness of Greece and especially of Athens was due to the fact that city-states could be so devoted to Beauty that they lived and died for it. This could well have been the center of their concept of *Arētē*, that indefinable center of virtue which every Athenian sought to achieve above all other things.

There are some subsidiary data which suggest such a conclusion. One is that Helen as an individual does not figure in the art of Ancient Greece. In the Greek sections in the museums I have gone through in Europe, and the many times I have been in the National Museum in Athens, I have never seen a statute or bas-relief of Helen. Furthermore, the Greeks called themselves Hellenes, and the land is called Hellas to this day,·which indicates that Helen could really have been the symbolic figure for the soul of Greece. The Greek people were fighting for their inner selves which surely makes more sense than fighting for a flag. If this line of reasoning is sound, that the Greeks waged this war for "beauty in the inward man," as Socrates phrased it, we see some reason for the grandeur that was Greece. Any nation which can fight, and win, such battles for their own souls, for their belief in Beauty, deserves in some way to have the glory that is universally accorded this little, ancient nation.

Art is our way of managing our inner turmoil, transcending our terror, and protecting ourselves from our own psychotic tendencies. From the high tension of Motherwell's canvases, to the eruption of Hofmann's brilliant colors, to the despair of Picasso's *Guernica*, art relieves our extremes of emotion. Our inordinate passion is drained off; our pressure to act out these emo-

184

tions in society is relieved, and we are deeply consoled. Art gives us repose and harmony where there otherwise would be explosion and destruction. Thus art is our universal therapist. It mirrors and gives us catharsis for our terror of dehumanization. As we stand in the presence of de Kooning's canvases, we are strengthened in our efforts to transcend our inner conflicts. Modern art speaks often directly to our subconscious and preconscious selves, as in Pollock and Rothko. Instead of running from our troublesome dreams, we can welcome them into awareness, as when we look at Hofmann or Dali.

In these ways myth as an art form ministers to us on dimensions below consciousness; it encompasses our irrationality and our daimonic tendencies. Myths thus humanize mankind even though this process is always precarious. Thus myths give us a harmony of rational and irrational, a harmony of antimonies. Myths carry health-giving catharsis, as no one can doubt after seeing a performance of Sophocles' _Oedipus Rex_ or Aeschylus' _Agamemnon_. If we wished an explanation for humankind's invention of myths, we need go no farther than the fact that myths enable us to live more humanly in the midst of our unhuman, warring unconscious. Myths enable us to exist and persevere as strangers in a strange land.

# CHAPTER XI

# Modern Art AND THE Future

*In the Middle Ages we have art for God's sake,*
*in the Renaissance we have art for man's sake,*
*in the nineteenth century we have art for art's sake,*
*and in the twentieth century*
*we have no art for God's sake.*

G.K. CHESTERTON

## II

N 1922 two literary events happened that will leave their mark on this whole century. One was the publication of T.S. Eliot's "The Wasteland," in which these lines appeared:

> And I will show you something different from either
>   Your shadow at morning striding behind you,
>   Or your shadow at evening rising to meet you
>   I will show you fear in a handful of dust. . . .
>
> A crowd flowed over London Bridge, so many,
>   I had not thought death had undone so many.

What followed the publication of Eliot's poem, and what I believe Eliot was predicting, was the "wasteland" of our culture, the disintegration of the world we all had known and counted on, the Jazz Age, The Great Depression, the Dust Bowl and World War II. Nobody knew it would happen then—except the artists. I doubt even if T.S. Eliot would have known it consciously. But he knew it unconsciously, i.e., with the genius of the poet, when he wrote this poem. It is woven around the medieval myth of the wasteland and its impotent king. Eliot pictures our age as a wasteland in which the king has lost his potency and hence cannot procreate, a land in which no crops can grow, a land that is wasting away. The king is powerless to do anything about it. The whole poem is a fantastic prophecy—by common consent one of the great classics.

In the same year, 1922, *The Great Gatsby* by F. Scott Fitzgerald appeared. Several films were made of this novel which I think were travesties; they missed the whole point of the story. Actually *The Great Gatsby* is a prediction of the demise of the American Dream, the dream that everybody can get rich like Horatio Alger. In this novel Fitzgerald draws the picture of a man who believes he can make himself over into anything he wishes; he "sprang from his Platonic conception of himself." He had a "ferocious indifference to the drums of his destiny, to destiny itself." At one point Gatsby cries incredulously, "Can't repeat the past? . . . Why of course you can!" He believed he could do anything, he worshipped change, with no regard for destiny or society. Here is a man who believed in positive thinking with a vengeance. He lived by the belief that destiny and determinism had no place in his world. The novel ends in a crashing tragedy—a tragedy which the human potential movement and the New Age people have not yet appreciated, even in the 1980's. We do not realize that the Horatio Alger myth is dead, and art is trying to show us the demise of this dream.

We are now in a transitional period similar to that of the death of Hellenism and the birth of Roman arts and culture. It is a period also like the demise of medieval art and the birth of the Renaissance. In all transitional periods there is a confusion as to what the new meaning of art is going to be. Our period is especially difficult since we are in the very midst of that confusion. Werner Heisenberg remarks that the confusion in physics, just before the Einsteinian and Quantum theories were born to throw light on the whole of physics, is like the present confusion in art. I do not agree with his order—I think the artist is the predictor of what happens in science rather than the reverse—but his point about the confusion in art is surely accurate.

When any new culture is established, the art gives the people their language. In the Middle Ages all peasants knew the meaning of the figures in the stained glass of the windows of Chartres; this was their language. Chartres consists of a vast library of dazzling symbols and myths, and these constituted the life of the peasants. It was literally true that no sculptor or painter of stained glass needed to sign his works—God could see all and He would know. Similarly in the Renaissance, the new humanism made the new humanistic art recognizable to all. At this moment, we are in the midst of a new cultural transition with its attendant difficulties and confusion.

When giving the inaugural address at the opening of
a new wing in the Modern Museum in New York, Paul
Tillich spoke on the topic, "The Art of No Art." Though
we can surely understand what Chesterton and Tillich
meant, the problem, strictly speaking, is not "no art."
It is rather a confusion in our day of many different
forms of art. In the Metropolitan Museum, for example,
we pass through the rooms of Renaissance art and see a
similarity in colors and in forms. In the seventeenth
century we see portraits, like those by Van Dyck, running the whole length of the hall. In the early nineteenth century we see many landscapes and seascapes,
which became art of the kind taught in academia. At
the end of the nineteenth century we see protests against
academic art in Van Gogh, in Gauguin, in Cézanne and
in Picasso. By the art we can recognize the period it
comes from.

But in our contemporary age we have every kind of
art—Wyeth and his realism, de Kooning and his jagged
strokes which show great vitality and color with con-
torted figures, Motherwell and Franz Kline who reveal
the great tension in modern times. There is Tobey with
his calligraphy, Picasso who seemed to change his style
every decade, Pollock who painted with surprisingly
harmonious colors the abstract forms by means of his
"drip school," Olitski with his subconscious forms expressed in coat after coat of different colors with the
underlying pinks and lavendars showing through to produce a captivating charm, Rothko with his profundity
in which the deepest abstract forms of reality are available for those willing to meditate in the presence of his
paintings. There is Hans Hofmann with his energetic
and bright colors which seem to cry out with the vitality

192

and strength of the earth, O'Keeffe with her abstractions from nature. And so on and on.

The modern age reveals many different kinds of art with the basic form, the "soul" of modernity if I may say so, still undiscovered. Take Picasso. In his youth his draftsmanship was fantastically accurate in his paintings of peasants in Spain. Then in 1907 there broke forth cubism with his painting of "Les Demoiselles d'Avignon," a classic picture of nudes in a whorehouse. Just after the First World War he was painting figures of bathers that showed what *The Great Gatsby* meant, namely, we play, we have beautiful bodies, but it is going to amount to a meaningless tragedy. Then in the 1930s and early 1940s, Picasso painted pictures of machines. These were portraits not of persons but of the human being as a machine, with wheels, spokes, and so on; everyone seemed cold and made of steel. He didn't give these pictures names but rather numbers. Here is an artist predicting a century in which people will be taken over by computers, which is just what has actually happened.

In our trying to find meaning in such a transitional age, let us also refer to music. John Cage, the composer who has been very much in the forefront of modern music, was advertised as giving a concert in New York. There was an expectant crowd which filled the auditorium, but Cage ascended the platform and sat down at the piano for an hour, not lifting a finger. I think it tremendously important that here is a musician who thinks art is so crucial, and his music so significant, that he believes that before anyone can really hear it, they have to learn to listen to the silence.

What does this have to do with modern art? In this

book I take my stand as best I can with modern artists. I very deeply appreciate their work. But I think we have to realize that what they're trying to express often is a great emptiness, or sorrow and despair as in Picasso's *Guernica*. When you see a picture entitled "White on White," there is nothing on the canvas as far as you can discern. It was painted in two kinds of white and then framed. I am told that the modern artist Duchamp framed a toilet seat and hung it up as a picture. Like "White on White," there are other offerings which consist of paintings with a little dot here and there, or a couple of lines in the corner, and then framed. When I go into the National Gallery in Washington, I see several great Leonardo da Vincis and Rembrandts and a number of other works for all time. Then I come to the contemporary artists, and I have a feeling of coldness. Their paintings contain nothing about human beings that we can recognize. What these contemporary artists are basically trying to say is that one must *look*, and often times we see a very bleak future. Their prediction is not about the lovely country of America where everyone is going to get rich. It's a country that is becoming more and more mechanical, computerized, more and more money-occupied, directed by the Dow Jones Index— more and more humanly empty. Many of these artists, like the ones who draped cow's intestines and blood over a rusty automobile as a still life in front of my office building in New York a few years ago, are trying to say to people "Look! Really *look*, See what's happening, Take it in!"

Mark Rothko, whose Chapel is in Houston, was one of the great figures in modern art. He committed suicide, but before he died he wrote a letter explaining his sadness at the reception of his works. He felt that people could not understand what he was trying to do, that any rich man could buy up all his paintings, dig a hole in his back yard, and dump his canvases in to bury them from the world. Now to somebody who had had a passion all his life to communicate by way of art, to say something important to his fellow human beings, this prospect was a great tragedy indeed.

What there is in Rothko is color after color—red, black, then perhaps brilliant gold and then a coat of black and another of brown. Your initial feeling in that chapel might be dismal. Your second thought might be that to understand it requires a great deal of looking. Then you might sit on one of the benches in the chapel (which Rothko also designed) and you too would _look_. After a while you would begin to feel that here is someone speaking to you out of subterranean levels, speaking out of his depths to those who will listen; he is the psalmist crying, "Out of the depths I call unto Thee."

In a biographical film about Rothko, he is quoted as saying that when people look at his pictures, he hopes "They will laugh or cry or maybe pray." These words are very relevant. People sometimes laugh and walk out again, and they sometimes cry. When they begin to take in what goes on with an artist like Rothko, then perhaps they pray. That is very fitting for this chapel.

I have known a particular artist, Jules Olitski, for some twenty years, and I count him as my friend. His summer studio is on an island, where he has built a great barn. There are canvases all over the floor. Olitski paints with a mop and spray gun. The mop has a white flap at the end like the kind one uses in mopping a bank floor. He dips the mop into big pails of paint and then spreads it on the canvases. There are a number of levels in each painting; it is a mirage of many different colors. When you look at it you not only feel these basic patterns of curving physical forms, but you also begin to see the many different hues shining through. The more you look at it, the more colors you see which were covered up and are now reflected through the painting. As you let yourself gaze upon these canvases, you are rewarded with a rich visual experience and with the ecstasy which accompanies such an experience.

What these artists are trying to tell us, what they're predicting, it seems to me, is that we are at the end of an age. I am not a great lover of our present hedonistic age and our materialistic society, where "necessity is associated with horror and freedom with boredom," as Auden puts it:

> . . . . this stupid world where
> Gadgets are gods and we go on talking,
> Many about much, but remain alone,
> Alive but alone, belonging—where?—
> Unattached as tumbleweed.

I think our society is radically faulty in a number of ways—such as our amoral economic system, our loss of values, our vulnerability to nuclear war, the millions starving while wheat rots in our storage bins. The results are that the quality of human relationships has diminished. It is difficult for people in our day to see beyond the glamour, the sensational advances in science and medicine, the technological ease with computers, the *fata morgana* appearances of progress on all sides—yes, it is indeed difficult to see the reality underneath.

196

Perhaps the most powerful demonstration of my thesis is that our age is witnessing the diminishing of the teaching of humanities in our high schools and our colleges. After an intensive study of the humanities over the last six years, the National Endowment for the Humanities in Washington reported that these subjects are progressively being erased from college curricula. The humanities were originally the soul of educational institutions, and students learned about the perennial questions of human life through the great works of history, literature, philosophy and art. But now students can graduate from seventy-two percent of the colleges in the country without even taking modern or ancient history, that is, without any understanding of Greece and Rome, where our civilization came from, or our struggles since the Renaissance, or the wars that have put us in the present predicament of having our very existence threatened by nuclear war. It used to be pointed out when one entered college, that to learn a foreign language was to go into the heart of another people's culture, and understand its art and psyche. Now a student in the majority of colleges can go through without understanding any other people's culture, or any profession except his own.

I recall that I stumbled into a class in the ancient Greek language in Oberlin College and, in spite of being a country boy who scarcely knew Greece had ever existed, I remained in the class. It turned out to be the richest, most valuable class I ever took. Nowadays there are very few such classes that one can even stumble into.

Literature, which is the language which crosses all borders—the Russians Tolstoy and Dostoyevsky, the

French Proust, the German Goethe, the English Shakespeare, the Americans Emerson and Whitman—all these are now scantily studied, or not at all in the hurry to get on to the study of computers and business. And as far as the classics go—these great ancient Greek dramas and myths which are buried in our own souls, along with Dante's *Divine Comedy* and Marlowe's *Dr. Faustus*—these classics are not read at all by the majority of graduates. The understanding of the psyche of modern Americans requires knowing the self-interpretation of human beings in symbols and myths down through the ages; yet I rarely meet in my teaching graduate students who are planning to become psychotherapists, any who have even read the great classics.

The purpose of the humanities is to make us more human, to enrich our lives, to develop our imaginations, and to make life worth living. And it is a saddening thing that these subjects are being dismissed.

We need have no prejudice against engineering, business studies, accounting, techniques of all sorts including the use of computers, when we point out that these are studies of the *how* of life, to the neglect of *what* life is about. This is reflected in the fact that a professor of literature, so I am told by a professor-friend at one of our most distinguished universities, receives about thirty thousand dollars a year and a professor of business receives about eighty thousand.

Philosophy, which used to be concerned with understanding the meaning of life, is now defunct on most campuses or, where it still exists, it has capitulated to the technical trends by becoming analytical philosophy. These studies of techniques are concerned with *quantities*, with exchange of goods, money, and even the auctioning off of great pictures. But the humanities are concerned with the quality, the *what* of life, the painting of the pictures or the composing and playing of music.

The humanities are concerned, as I have said, with the questions of meaning. When, during the last century, they put on a great celebration in Boston at the completion of the stringing of telephone wires from Maine to Texas, Thoreau said, "Nobody asks the real question, Do the people of Maine have anything to say to the people of Texas?" Our age is replete with techniques for mass communication, but what is the content of what we communicate beyond business and money matters? Barbara Tuchman wrote a penetrating article in the *New York Times* two years ago entitled, "The Decline of Quality." When I had it xeroxed and passed around, a number of people were offended: how dare she criticize our great age of mass communication, our new techniques for everything from TV to dish-washing? This, of course, was exactly what she meant: the quality of life diminishes as the concern with quantity burgeons.

This of course has a great deal to do with modern art and the future. Art—in which we include along with painting and sculpture, the dance, architecture, literature, poetry, music—is devoted to the quality of human life. Hence the great confusion in art in our time: it is as though art is lost, it has no central soul or direction in which to go.

But we note at the same time the poignant hunger of people for great art as shown in the crowds that line up to see the exhibitions of the artifacts of King Tut, or the works of Picasso or Van Gogh. Of course one can argue that this is conformism; people crowd in because that is the thing to do. But I do not believe such arguments exhaust the motives. Men and women do not live by bread alone—even if cake with a hundred flavors is added. It is a genuine hunger, a starvation for what people's own intuition tell them is great. It is the artists, the musicians, the poets, the dramatists that remind us that life *is* worth living. Some of us can say with truth that beauty has saved our lives, especially if we are talking about life abundant.

In transitional ages there is bound to be some kind of cultural breakdown. The whole society becomes disoriented and negates itself. When we fail to see this from a historical viewpoint, then we do get hopeless, pessimistic, and lose our sense of balance—for we know only the present that will be destroyed in the cultural change. This illustrates again the dangers we face in dropping history—along with the other humanities—from college curricula.

We can, however, experience ourselves as part of a culture that is dying in order that a new society may be born. This dying period is certainly no picnic for any sensitive person. Psychological breakdowns are almost the "normal" thing in our day; we have psychotherapists of all kinds trying to meet this need. But for the most part therapists are equipped only to patch people up. The breakdowns of our morals and family life—all these are part of the radical change. If we can see it that way, then we can move ahead with courage. We can realize that we are building a future, trying to produce some context, some art, some drama, some music that will communicate something to future ages. That I would like to be part of. And I'm sure all of us would.

Now we return specifically to the role of modern art in this transition. Joseph Binder, my teacher in Vienna during the summers of 1932–33, helped us here when he continually urged us, as I have mentioned, to "find the ground form." His advice could be translated, "Get below the surface, below all your superficial whims and find the reality, the foundation. Find the structure on which your life is built." This simple counsel is surely a central part of modern art.

One summer on the coast of Maine, John Marin made several of his watercolors. These paintings were done with Marin's characteristic style—a dash across the sky for clouds, a jagged blue and brown expressing the ocean, strong vertical lines of green for spruce trees and the curves of brownish-red showing the unpredictable might of this rugged, rock-bound coast. Each stroke of Marin's brush is made with profound emotion. When he had completed these particular paintings he took them into the drug store in the little town and stood them against the wall. He then asked the pharmacist, whom we all knew as a typical "Down Easterner," how he liked them. The druggist answered, "They'll be fine when they're finished."

What the druggist called "unfinished" was really the genius of Marin; he "looked on beauty bare," as Edna St. Vincent Millay said of Euclid. In every transitional age one must let go the finishing, and look on beauty bare. The incompleteness, the groping, fits our age. Our beauty is not at all "pretty" or "charming"—it may be the bare rock, the skeleton watercolors of Marin, the silence of John Cage sitting at his piano without a note, the discord and sound of cultures grinding together.

It is dangerous to look if you are not prepared. Hence

Plato, as Greece began its deterioration, wrote of the *terror* of beauty, and Rilke wrote these enigmatic lines:

> For beauty is nothing but the beginning of terror
> which we still are just able to endure and we are
> so awed because it serenely disdains to annihilate
> us.

We have in music, especially in the giants like Beethoven and Schönberg, the same sense of terror. And even Dostoyevsky, who certainly knew what beauty was, has Dmitri, one of his characters in the *Brothers Karamazov*, cry out,

> The awful thing is that beauty is mysterious as well
> as terrible. God and the devil are fighting there
> and the battlefield is the heart of man.

Yes, this is what modern art is all about. It has little or nothing to do with prettiness or niceness or sweetness. In its beauty there is the terror of the ground forms, and the contemporary artists are our "distant early warning." They tell us of the fundamentals of love and the terror of life and of death.

# CHAPTER XII

# *Ecstasy*
## AND *Violence*

*What is man before beauty*
*liberates him from free pleasure,*
*and the serenity of forms*
*tames down the savageness of life?*

FRIEDRICH VON SCHILLER

# 12

LATE ONE afternoon in September not many years ago, a friend and I left a Swiss border town and drove up through the foothills of the French Alps toward Chamonix and Mt. Blanc. For the first two hours we could see nothing except spruce trees as the road wound through the forests of the foothills. Then suddenly coming out on a plateau, we were startled to see to the southeast the whole sky filled with an orange-pink mountain range. There were two peaks, not Mt. Blanc itself but the mountains between us and Mt. Blanc. The sun was setting and the snow-covered range reflected and radiated its color from the rays of the sun behind us. It was so breath-taking that we stopped our car to gaze at it for a while; we felt as though we were bathing in a sky turned into sheer brilliance.

We arrived in Chamonix after dark. Our room in the inn had a large picture window to the southeast, and in the darkness we could see the vast dark lines of Mt. Blanc, silent lord of the entire horizon. On the windowsill of the room was the customary box of geraniums which made a foreground over which we could feel and dimly see the presence of the great mountain.

The next morning I sat on the windowsill for half an hour intensely concentrating on the mountain peak. I cleared my mind of everything and held my gaze steadily on the great cone of glowing snow. As I gazed for the first part of the half hour, Mt. Blanc remained a realistic mountain, pure ivory white, incredibly beautiful against the deep blue of the morning sky.

Then, as I continued to concentrate on it, the mountain gradually changed before my eyes into another form. It became abstract. It was now, as the underlying form emerged, composed of disembodied squares and circles and planes. I loved it still, as I love the cubist paintings by Picasso and Braque in the first decade of this century. The mountain form seemed to be painted on a canvas, it was disembodied, pure form with no weight or movement. Or one could as easily say, the mountain form was all weight and all movement; with living form it does not matter, as Brancusi illustrates in his sculptures of a golden line soaring up from its base which he rightly calls "Bird in Flight."

But as I continued to concentrate steadily on it, this weightless form gradually changed again. The vast mountain took on a body, now organic, three-dimensional. It became a new being on a new level. Now I saw it in a living depth. The glowing ivory forms had come together again into an organism, not personal but

206

neither was it impersonal. It seemed to be pure form. I felt more than saw an embodied structure, now an ultimate form, part of the universe as I was also. The mountain, like myself looking at it, embodied a universe of beauty and meaning.

Since that day, this experience of my concentration on Mt. Blanc has remained vivid in my mind. Back in New York, later, when I looked out the window of my office on the 25th floor high above the Riverside Drive, I saw in the delicate skyline of New York also pure form—now pure lace. The clouds above the city likewise assumed the forms I had seen in Chamonix, and as I walked home at night the giant elm trees on Riverside Drive took on this same significant form, all part of the same universe.

This experience of living forms, this embodied being, took me out of myself. Whenever I called it out of the past and into my mind again, it gave me a new experience which was beyond living or dying. The feeling was oceanic, as Freud or Einstein would say; it was my participation in the Being of the universe.

Such an experience cannot be said to exist only in my imagination, nor is it solely a kind of "telepathy" emerging from Mt. Blanc. The experience is both inner and outer, both subjective and objective. It is a fusion of my imagination and the emanating form of the mountain.

This is an illustration of ecstasy. The word comes from the Greek _ex-stasis_, meaning to stand outside of, or above. It is also self-transcendent. It gives one the experience of going beyond, or absorbing the old self, and a new self, or more accurately an enlarged self, takes its place. To put it in psychoanalytic language, my ego was not denied but absorbed. My self was enlarged by participation in a new being which happened in this case to be the form of Mt. Blanc.

My letting go of my ordinary awareness, which I call my banal consciousness, permitted a new consciousness to be born in me. Eastern religion and philosophy speak of this as the experience of the Absolute, or "cosmic experience," a participation in a "universal awareness." One participates in a greater consciousness, temporarily as it may be.

You will probably be aware, as you read this, that I am also talking of the consciousness of the artist. Artists are the ones who are particularly sensitive to experiencing scenes in new forms. They have the capacity to look at a scene until it is born in their inner minds and imagination, born in their total consciousness. This may occur immediately, as the artists look at a scene for the first time, or it may be a new experience of a scene they have already seen many times, like Monet's waterlilies.

This is what people mean when they say, "I've looked at this many times, but this is the first time I've really *seen* it." I have looked at many trees in my life, but I never really *saw* one until I had seen Cézanne's paintings of trees. Through participating in Cézanne's imagination, which so unforgettably finds the "ground forms" of trees, I was enabled to experience and create for myself the form of trees in a new and completely different way. This is one of the contributions artists make to the world: they experience these living forms, and through their art they enable the rest of us to see them—or better to *experience* them in our lives.

The artists, including any and all of us who choose to create, to "make" imaginatively, are the ones who bare themselves to this experience of essence. They are the ones who are caught up in greater or lesser ecstasy, and they hasten then to reproduce it on paper or on canvas or in music. Their vocation is to communicate that experience to others. Not to communicate it is to surrender the vision to atrophy; the artist must paint, or write, or sculpt—else the vision withers away and he or she is less apt to have it again.

There is also another accompaniment to this experience of ecstasy, and that is gratitude. I think I have never painted a watercolor, sketchy as it might have been, without feeling a strange gratification afterwards. I sometimes feel I have been invited in where angels fear to tread, and for that who would not be grateful? The wonder of being human is that any of us who so choose may be privileged to participate in this experience of ecstasy, with its accompanying gratitude.

*Ecstasy and Self-Transcendence*

As I have described ecstasy and self-transcendence, one can understand why some people yearn to remain in that state all the time. The delicious feelings of self-transcendence are set loose in different ways by music which we love, by poetry which activates long thoughts and deep feelings, as well as in painting and the other arts.

If such ecstasy is as joyful, as reassuring, as soul cleansing as I have indicated, why not live with the "Absolute" all the time? Why not stay on the level of ecstasy and beauty and self-transcendence perpetually and forever? This self that seems at times to be the repository of all the "garbage" that goes on in one's mind, this ego which seems to be the root of anxiety

and guilt feeling and despair—why not stay always on
the level where these undesirable and unpleasant centers of feeling are wiped away? Why not transcend one's
ugly self all the time?

The answer is simple. Because ecstasy and self-
transcendence are also the source of violence, destruction, wars and hatred as well as these noble things I
have mentioned.

The transcendence of the self gives us not only the
delicious feelings, but also sadness, yearning, anger and
all other emotions. We know how Hitler was able to set
loose through martial music the emotions which led to
the most violent of World Wars. The emotions are stim-
ulated for good or evil, and we are loosed from our customary banality. We have only to call to mind the great
communal ecstasy shared by over a hundred thousand
young persons in Woodstock, New York in the summer
of 1969.

Let us take from psychotherapy a more systematic
example of self-transcendence leading to violence. The
following case, referred to in my book *Power and Innocence*, occurred in the early '70's in New York City. A
patient who was a doctoral student at a university participated in a march on Wall Street to protest the Vietnam War. This march was attacked not only by the police but also by construction workers employed on a new
building. In his subsequent therapy hour, he described
the experience as follows.

> I had a spontaneous feeling, I was caught up in
> something above human desires. We all were to-
> gether in a great cause. Business as usual was thrown
> aside. You forget your bodily needs and cares, you
> channel everything through the group, the group

210

becomes the most important thing. . . . But the group was leaderless, it was milling aimlessly about. I saw the construction workers down one street getting prepared to throw bricks at us. I tried to cry out to the group, "Go down this other street instead!"

(A little later in that hour) The group was milling aimlessly about when someone shouted, "Let's get the computer!" All my life I've wanted to smash a computer. Now someone else was doing it—that made it great, it was justifiable.

(Later) It's hard to talk in here about personal problems at a time like this.

Quite apart from the right or wrong of this movement or its success or failure, or the Luddite uselessness of smashing computers, it is clear that this young man was caught up in a self-transcendence that each of us can identify with. He felt the cause was greater than his usual self, something he could surrender to; and he got a strong sense of unity or bonding with his fellows; he no longer needed to take responsibility for himself. During those days in therapy he was the "healthiest," most "normal" (if I may use these threadbare words) of any time until then. His feeling of wanting to do violence was justified by the group; it was a time like war, when all the primitive desires of being human come out and are justified and rationalized by patriotism, the self-transcendence of the whole group.

Thus self-transcendence is neither good nor evil in itself. It is an experience beyond good and evil, in Nietzsche's words. I have pointed out in *Power and Innocence* that war itself, the most destructive form of hu-

211

man violence, is also a time of ecstasy and self-transcendence. J. Glen Gray, a captain in the last war for two years in the front lines before he became an intelligence officer for the American Forces, later re-visited Europe on a Fulbright grant to study the attitudes of the people who had participated in the war. To his considerable surprise, he found that families he had known in such war-ravaged countries as France now missed the sense of adventure, the banding together against a common enemy, the sense of "being caught up in something above human desire," as my patient had put it. They missed the challenge of being devoted to a cause greater than themselves. Among Glen Gray's comrades in the resistance movement of fifteen years before, a French woman, living in her comfortable bourgeois home with her husband and son, confessed earnestly and somewhat apologetically, "My life is so utterly boring nowadays! . . . . Anything is better than to have nothing at all happen day after day. You know that I do not love war or want it to return. But at least it made me feel alive, as I have not felt alive before or since."

Glen Gray goes on about another comrade-in-arms, who was overweight and smoking an expensive cigar, speaking of their previous days together when he was shivering and hungry and harried with anxieties about his wife and children, "Sometimes I think that those were happier times for us than these." And there was something like despair in his eyes. . . . Neither one of these people was longing for the old days in sentimental nostalgia; they were confessing their disillusionment with a sterile present. *Peace exposed a void in them that war's excitement had enabled them to keep covered up.* They lacked the ecstasy and self-transcendence, to put it in our terms, which war had given them.

212

A veteran of the Vietnam war, William Broyles, wrote in *Esquire* (November, 1984) an article entitled "Why Men Love War." In it, Broyles quotes his fellow soldiers whom he met at the Vietnam Veterans' Memorial in Washington, "What people cannot understand is how much fun Vietnam was. I loved it. I loved it, and I can't tell anybody." Broyles is describing again the adventure, the sense of community, the intense bonding with fellowmen, the zest of risking everything—all experiences of ecstasy and self-transcendence.

The banding together into a great unity, the sense of transcending individual desires, the freedom from personal responsibility—all these aspects of war are clearly conducive to ecstasy and self-transcendence. No wonder William James wrote in his classic essay, "The Moral Equivalent of War," that in our anti-war campaigns we are self-defeating in emphasizing the horror of war; for "the horror is part of the fascination." We who are opposed to war need a new approach, James went on, that will set up positive ideals that bring the sense of adventure, the attraction, the sense of giving one's self to a cause more than "business as usual," if we are to succeed in our prevention of war.

A captain who was one of the teachers in the ROTC which I was required to take during my two years at Michigan State College once remarked in his lectures to the class, "You are told that war is hell. I never had such a good time in my life as I did in France during the last war." I looked at the man as though he were a pariah; but since then I have realized that he was saying something much more important than he knew. As long as this captain had to arise every morning and get dressed and shaved and drag himself over to the campus to drum some army tactics into the heads of five hundred students who did not want to hear, he—and the millions of people who likewise have no sense of zest in life—will dream about the adventure and excitement of this most destructive form of human violence. War, the epitome of destruction as it is, and the threat to our total planet that it is in our day of nuclear war, nevertheless gives a sense of ecstasy and self-transcendence that is prized by millions of people.

For people cannot stand to be of no significance. And ecstasy and the self-transcendence which goes with war and violence lift one out of this feeling of insignificance. Psychotics show this need for significance in such obvious things as insisting they are Napoleon or Christ, or that they have a special relationship with Jupiter or other constellations in the heavens. Neurotics show it in a less obvious way. But there is, however it is shown, still the powerful drive to demonstrate "I amount to something, I will be missed if I commit suicide. I will take drugs to be whisked into a state where I have no more guilt and despair, and I feel only my own significance."

Terrorism and the whole drug scene are vivid examples of the fact that what persons abhor most of all in life is the possibility that they will not matter. John Wilkes Booth would be a name long since erased in history, but he shot Lincoln and therefore he will be known as long as anyone can read a history book. If Hinckley had succeeded in assassinating Reagan, he would indeed have proved to his imagined sweetheart that he was a man of consequence, someone to be reckoned with.

214

### Art as Antidote for Violence

One purpose of art, and the beauty which is its inspiration, is to counteract this experience of insignificance. People have to have a sense of transcendence of their boring, day-to-day existence, and to live with some adventure, joy, zest, and a sense of meaning and purpose in their existence.

Art is an antidote for violence. It gives the ecstasy, the self-transcendence that could otherwise take the form of drug addiction, or terrorism, or suicide or warfare. We have seen that both violence and art—and the beauty which is the center of art—yield the experience of ecstasy and self-transcendence. But art and violence are directly opposite in their effects.

We find, strangely enough, that the pursuit of art and beauty are what we have long sought, namely, the antidote to violence.

I propose that this is the function of beauty and art in human experience. I do not overlook the pressing need to correct the faults of our society—our gross nationalism, our making human beings subordinate to technology, our failure to value human rights above property rights, our racial and gender injustice. But I wish to go below these considerations, to a universal level where the sense of significance will be recognized as every person's right because he or she is part of a universe of beauty.

First, art has the capacity to prevent violence in such a way that the venom is taken out of the violence. This mysterious power is shown in its capacity to portray violence in forms that are a catharsis. Take, for example, Picasso's _Guernica_. This painting shows decapitated bulls, women impaled on the sword, babies on the end of spears. It is painted in black and grey, the most depressing colors in the spectrum. The whole picture is an expression of Picasso's grief, his rage and hopelessness at the bombing of the helpless little village of Guernica by Hitler's planes during the Spanish war for freedom. Depressing? Yes. But the strange effect as we leave after concentrating on the painting is a sense of compassion, an inner resolve that such violence must be curbed, and we join Picasso in his hatred for all of the experiences that he, in his extraordinary sensitivity, sees in the violence of our modern world.

Looking at *Guernica* makes us reaffirm our quality as human beings. It presents beauty even in this picture of the gross cruelty of human beings; and this beauty deepens our love for those who suffer. In this respect Picasso has the same effect as Shakespeare in his drama *King Lear*, or Aeschylus in *The Oresteia*, and other great tragedies of human history. *Guernica* is a catharsis; it presents man's inhumanity to man move vividly than reams of printed paper could do, and it presents the beauty which marks human beings in contrast to this gross cruelty.

Modern art often seems to me to be the area in which honesty is most forthright in presenting the violence in our society. Call to mind Ben Shawn and his pictures of the Sacco Vanzetti case, which did more to expose the miscarriage of justice in the execution of these two men than volumes of writing. Even the improvised sculpture I mentioned earlier, of the wrecked car with a cow's blood and intestines splashed over the seats, is gross indeed, but if one can empathize with the meaning of the artists, one sees a picture of the violence inherent in modern technology. Motherwell's work, expressing the tension and anxiety of modern life especially in his dashing black lines and strange black forms, also carries an underlying tone of violence turned into an experience of catharsis. Surely in de Kooning's jagged lines and well-chosen discords of color, there is also the violence of our day; and we do not need to emphasize the large dragon's teeth of his portraits of Marilyn Monroe and his other portraits of women to demonstrate this.

Art is catharsis. So Aristotle argued centuries ago. And so it is in our day and as long as human beings remain human.

The sketch of the gypsy girl, on the following page, expresses a suffering beyond her years and exemplifies how sadness takes on a new meaning when it is formed into art. The girl is obviously unhappy. Yet in the catharsis art can perform, the sketch gave me an ecstatic experience as I was making it, and gives us who now view it an attraction which is not sad at all. When viewing it we feel an empathy with her sadness, but also a catharsis in the sense that looking at it gives us a transcendence of its emotion. How interesting, also, that in her sadness she still puts lilacs in her hair!

Let us look intensively at one painting of the artist Adolph Gottlieb, called "Blast One." It is a relatively large oil now owned by the Modern Museum in New York. It consists of two huge forms on the canvas, one of jet black, and the other a large red-orange circle above the black. From one point of view the black is an image of destruction, discord, confusion—a presentation of the Hiroshimas and Nagasakis of recent history. The black seems to be twisted girders, masses of power shooting off in every direction, a conglomeration of once molten black steel. The tension between this black image of

217

Gypsy girl with lilacs in her hair,
drawn in central Greece, 1933.

destruction with the red circle above gives the picture its great power. This is surely violence as vivid as one can imagine.

But there is also the sun, the red-orange circle, painted over with many coats which adds to its depth. Yellow and all the light and warm shades add up to a powerful, radiant source of all heat and light. This is the dwelling of Phoebus Apollo. We recall that Apollo is also the god of order, form, rationality. The sun is poised above the nihilism, above the shifting darkness.

Thus the painting is a regeneration adjacent to the eternal void. The meaning it gives us lies in the power to renew existence. In our confronting the ultimate in anti-humanity—the nuclear blast—we see the power (which came originally from our sun, which is there also before us) to regenerate. Whether we survive as human or we start over on our primordial trek; whether it is on our planet or one of the other billions in the heavens, the regeneration goes on and on. It may be that the myth of Genesis will have to be re-enacted. But the painting tells that the artist's faith is that renewal goes on eternally.

This painting is a simple abstract image, with nothing cultural about it, and this very simplicity gives it power. The image implores us to be aware of the age-old conflict between the sun and the blackness, between _eros_ and _thanatos_, between the light and the great void. It is a primordial conflict, light triumphing over darkness, a conflict of good versus evil, "yes" versus "no," order versus revolution. This is precisely the conflict which give us consciousness in the first place. This dialectic struggle is what makes human beings human. It is the primordial tension between consciousness and unconsciousness.

As I look at Gottlieb's "Blast One," I find myself musing over the original cave paintings, in Altamira and Lascaux, those fascinating pictures of bright color and impeccable form which came in human history probably at the same time as human beings learned to think.

For art—and beauty the contemplation of which leads to art—is an inseparable part of our precious capacity to be conscious, to think. Art was invented, I surmise, out of the necessity of those original men and women to regenerate, to propagate, to renew the race of human-kind. Our dimensions of hope we now need to extend to include the other solar bodies; the hope that springs eternal in the human breast can include other planets and worlds. "Homo, called Sapiens," which Edna St. Vincent Millay wrote once mockingly, can be seen also as the truth that regeneration can go on forever.

# CHAPTER XIII

## *Beauty*
### OUR UNIVERSAL
## *Language*

*The new humanity will be universal,
and it will have the artist's attitude;
that is, it will recognize that the immense
value and beauty of the human being
lies precisely in the fact that he belongs
to the two kingdoms of nature and the spirit.*

THOMAS MANN

# *13*

URING A Christmas vacation while I was a teacher in Greece, I sailed to Egypt. It was about six o'clock in the evening and we were due to dock in Alexandria at midnight. Across the water I had already seen the dim outline of the mosques in that city, the minarets of which rose up into the sky as though eager to get the first view of every ship bound for its port.

But at this hour as the day bid us good-bye, several of the passengers were standing beside me at the ship's rail looking at an amazing sunset. The sky was luminous with two long streaks of light yellow clouds, lending a radiance against which the sun sank toward the sea. The great red-orange ball, getting larger as it neared the horizon, seemed to reach out too eagerly to make passionate contact with the waters of the Mediterranean. The path between the sun and our ship was like the molten fire of liquid rock pouring out of a volcano. Just as the sun seemed ready to dip below the horizon, it hesitated a moment and spread out its radiance as though to remind us of its mastery of our universe. Then suddenly it was gone, leaving behind a sky and sea painted with every kind of riotous red and lustrous yellow in every combination.

A well-dressed man stood next to me at the rail watching the sunset. From his tiny tailored moustache and his dark complexion I imagined that he was Turkish. He said something to me I did not understand, and we both smiled a little apologetically because I could speak no Turkish and he apparently knew no English. But we immediately recovered our dignity nodding toward the same sunset which captivated us both, a bond between us as we watched nature's brilliance overflow on to the profligate sea.

On the other side of me stood a blondish, older woman, perhaps in her early forties, with deep grey eyes and smooth features. I imagined her to be Scandinavian. But when she also smiled at me and murmured, *"Schön, schön,"* I knew she was German.

It was only later that I began to realize that these two persons, my companions in watching nature's magnificence, were supposed to be, according to my childhood conditioning, my enemies. The "terrible Turk" was a phrase I had picked up in my childhood when the Turks were massacring and starving the Armenians. The woman on my left belonged to the race which—so I had also

been taught as a very small child during World War I—
had cut off the breasts of Belgian women, and the next
few years her people, under Hitler, were to overrun
Europe again in contemporary madness. But here we
were standing together watching the beautiful natural
phenomenon of Apollo driving his chariot beyond the
western sea.

The strange thing about beauty is that it wipes away
all boundaries and inspires us to realize our common
humanity. Our destiny interweaves us with each other,
and our arts make every war nowadays a civil war, a war
against our brothers and sisters no matter what nation
they happen to belong to.

Beauty overcomes distinctions between all people on
this planet. In beauty we have a language common to
all of us despite racial or cultural differences—and even
despite national and historical enmities. For this very
Egypt, to which I was then traveling, later shared with
us in America the art objects found in King Tut's tomb,
and crowds of people stood in our twentieth-century lines
for hours for the privilege of seeing the statues in bronze
and gold which had been buried with this king in ancient Egypt. The colorful Turkish and Persian rugs which
decorate the floors of tens of thousands of persons in all
countries and have influenced the designs of rugs vir-
tually all over the world, came from the same part of
the world as the "terrible Turk" standing politely beside me. And when we think of the contribution of
German-speaking peoples—from Boehme to Beethoven
to Goethe to Hegel, *et al.*—our words fail us.

All these are our common heritage of beauty, and never
has there been any doubt that they belonged to all civilized people. No matter how primitive, the things of

beauty from Africa to Alaska, from China to Australia, from New York to India are the language of all beings who call themselves human.

*One Buys a Violet*

My mind goes back to those two summers in 1932 and 1933 when, as the International School of Art, we traveled, painting and drawing as we went, through the peasant villages of central Europe. The bright colors now come back to me: the brilliant red and magenta of each nationality, the blue and yellow of designs, different as they were from each other but in another sense all similar. In Hungary, the dark red skirts which spun outward as the dancers swung around in their peasant whirls, each woman and man adorned with black aprons embroidered with flowers in yellow and blue. Then in Czechoslovakia, the colors were lighter in pink and brilliant green, vests laced up the front, all embroidered through many winters of whiling away the daylight and snow-bound hours crocheting. The Polish mountaineers showed the same fondness for bright colors and homespun harmony, seemingly copied from the flowers every family had planted in their thatch-roofed house with its stork nests on its chimney. Everywhere the flowers were of similar varieties—sunflowers, lilies, hollyhocks, and many kinds I did not know. Everywhere the designs betokened a bond between the peasants, no matter what flag the Treaty of Versailles had placed them under.

What does it mean that these peasants used symbolic forms, cones, circles in their designs as they sewed costumes for a marriage ceremony or when they painted flowers on the walls of their huts? It was only later that I learned the advice of Cézanne to young painters to

226

"see nature in cones, rectangles, squares, circles," i.e. the forms that make up abstract art. But these peasants, knowing nothing of Cézanne, had for untold centuries seen nature in these same abstract forms, as though they were inwardly commanded to interpret their view of nature in precisely Cézanne's ways. When I looked at the designs on vases and drinking cups in Hungary or Poland, I recalled the friezes on the vases of ancient Greece which are the treasures of almost every museum in our civilized world.

What does it mean that everywhere we find human beings seeking art in the same kind of designs and forms, from the Navajo Indians of North America to the natives of Africa to ancient Greece to the peasants of Europe? What is this thirst, the yearning in all peoples which cannot be denied to make something which gives them delight? Is it to satisfy some unknown inner urge or to express objectively the way each peasant sees the world at its best? Or simply to brighten whatever corner he or she has and to make it livable? These peasants could not understand the language of their counterparts of other countries, but they could understand completely the language of designs on the vases which pleased their eyes everytime they used them. What does it mean that each of these nationalities of peasants develops its dance, unique but similar, to express their exhilaration and their hope for some happiness?

Some of these similarities may be the cultural influence from one country to another, but the fundamental need of human beings to ornament their vases and their tools is surely not. From the flowers of China on their light green vases to the cherry blossoms on Japanese parchment to the designs on holy manuscripts in Tibet, to the veils in India to the rugs in the near east woven to the songs of the leader, to the designs of the Navajo rings in the new world—everywhere we find human beings making ornaments on their clothes and armor and on everything that is meaningful to them. The ancient Greeks could not use a vase for oil or wine without painting in black on the terra-cotta red of the vase the stories of Sirens chasing some youth or chariot races with lovely horses or the stories of the gods in Homer, all so intricate and fascinating that it gives a person hours of delight tracing these tales in the Metropolitan Museum or in London or the Louvre or anywhere these vases are gathered.

Even the death-dealing swords and other armaments show the owners' love of design. The shields, the spears to protect one's self and to kill one's opponents, are covered with designs which tell the old Homeric tales over and over again. And in the majority of cases this beauty has nothing in the world to do with function or utility. Indeed, an unadorned sword or spear would pierce the heart of the enemy more easily.

The ancient Persian saying seems to be true for all of us, "If I have one penny, with half of it I buy some bread, and with the other half I buy a violet."

Perhaps even more puzzling is the fact that the primitive art—which our peasants in central Europe and their ceremonies richly demonstrated—has had such a pronounced influence on contemporary artists in New York City and London and Paris. Primitive art, the carved wood and painted totems from Africa to Alaska, from China to Australia, from New York to India, is the language a multitude of modern artists speak. It seems that whenever art in our capital cities becomes dried up, exhausted in principle, reduced to copying previous masters, the artists are driven back to find again the primitive sources of beauty, to drink again the inspiration from the original forms of circle and cube and the language which Gauguin and Van Gogh and their colleagues found. They find again what friends in the art world call "honest" forms; they drink again and deeply of the Pierian Springs.

We realize now that our common human language is not Esperanto or computers or something having to do with vocal cords and speech. It is, rather, our sense of proportion, our balance, harmony and other aspects of simple and fundamental form. Our universal language, in other words, is beauty.

Beneath our loquacious chatter, there is a silent language of our whole being which yearns for art and the beauty from which art comes. For we find ourselves an integral part of this universe in our breathing, our heart beat, our amazing balance in such a minor thing as taking one step on the path: the earth comes up to meet us, as Newton pointed out, that infinitesimally small distance, and our foot goes out to meet the earth. From this fantastic balance of the human organism comes the art of walking and ultimately to making such forms as the ballet dancers which Degas shows us in his rich paintings. When Kant said, "Two things incline the heart to wonder, the starry sky above and the moral law within," I wish to add a third. That is the amazing sense of balance that enables us to walk and run and to dance in the ways the peasants and other humans celebrate and express their ecstasy in all parts of the world.

Art is the instrument by which beauty is actualized. Art is the eternal endeavor to realize beauty. Sometimes it is successful, sometimes a failure; but the poignancy of beauty will never let us go.

As I write I fantasize that God had added an eleventh commandment, which Moses kept secret because he thought it would conflict with the second commandment which prohibited graven images, since the Hebrews were living among idolatrous tribes. This suppressed eleventh commandment was "Thou shalt make thyself and thy world beautiful, for this is why I sent my gardeners, Adam and Eve, to cultivate the flowers in Eden. And this is why I have made the twilights and the springtime so radiant with splendor."

And I fantasize that this is why Joan of Arc cried out from the stake when she was being burnt, "How long! O Lord, how long will it take for thy people to see thy presence in this beautiful earth?"

*Beauty and Literature*

We find a similar truth in the great literature of the world. Whether one's native speech is French or Urdu or Chinese or any other, the literature of the world—if only in translation—is open to us all. We never think of avoiding reading Goethe because he is German, or that Shakespeare is confined to Britain, or that the Koans are the property only of the Japanese. The more deeply authors penetrate into the depths of human experience the more they speak the language of all humanity. They then give solace and enhancement to all of us. This is another definition of a classic: a writing that interprets our own deepest symbols and myths. Hence a classic passes on from ancient Homer, say, to all of us no matter how many centuries later we may live and no matter what nationality we may be.

230

The drama, *Peer Gynt,* for example, is entirely about the question, "What is my Self?," surely the deepest puzzle of human beings in whatever country. When Ibsen wrote the drama he thought his play would not be understood outside Scandinavia. But to his surprise he found that Peer was understood wherever human beings were conscious of themselves, wherever human beings asked, "Where is myself?"; and hence Peer was claimed everywhere as a national prototype.

Even in Japan it was stated that Peer Gynt "is typically Japanese." George Bernard Shaw wrote that "The universality of Ibsen (and his grip upon humanity) makes his plays come home to all nations, and Peer Gynt is as good a Frenchman as a Norwegian." There is on my desk a copy of the book of poems by the contemporary Russian poet, Yevgeny Yevtushenko. Opening the book at random I found these lines,

> The visions of malapaga
> those of Peer Gynt,
> seem, all of them, now
> to apply to me.

The reason Peer Gynt is a character for all nations is that the myth and the drama reflect on a profound level the problems, the loves, the yearnings, the sorrows, the ultimate discoveries of one human being who stands for all human beings. After reading it, we arise from our chairs feeling deeply understood; our loneliness is assuaged and our hearts feel at home again. Such a classic gives us a sense of joy and serenity—which after all is our definition of beauty.

Poetry is a particular form of art which gives us another aspect of beauty in our common human language.

One may ask one's self, Why is it that so many of the great classics in human history are written in poetry? Homer's *Iliad* and *Odyssey*, Lucretius's *The Nature of Things*, Aeschylus's *Agamemnon*, Vergil's *Aeneid*, Shakespeare's dramas, Goethe's *Faust* are all in poetry. One might think that prose would be more flexible, and therefore enable the writer to range more widely than in poetry. But no: depth rather than flexibility is what these authors seek, and poetry requires a deeper level of communication.

Dante's *Divine Comedy*, for example, begins with these two verses:

> Midway in our life's journey, I went astray
> from the straight road and woke to find myself
> alone in a dark wood. How shall I say

> what wood that was! I never saw so drear,
> so rank, so arduous a wilderness!

Thus begins what is certainly one of the most human, richest and beautiful classics that we humans are heir to, no matter what our language. In exile from Florence for political reasons, Dante found his personal hardship turned into a great gift to humanity. He wrote this epic not only in poetry but in what would seem to be the most arduous kind of poetry. Each of the three parts, the *Inferno*, *Purgatorio*, and *Paradiso*, consists of thirty-three Cantos, each one of which is made up of forty or fifty three-line verses. Each of the Cantos ends in the word "Star": "And we walked out once more beneath the Stars" ends the first book, "perfectly pure, and ready for the Stars" the second, and the third, "by the love that moves the Sun and the other Stars."

It would seem that such architectonics would make the _Comedy_ rigid and hard to read. But it does just the opposite. The piercing of human experience so deeply that it can be expressed only in poetry means pushing one's thoughts to a deeper form. A tension is required to write such poetry, and this tension in turn requires the poet to express his thoughts on a deeper level of art.

I have said earlier that art is arriving at form in human life. The fact that the poet, in this case Dante, confronts the cadence, the sense of proportion, the form of poetry, requires Dante's feeling for the depths of the human soul. Poetry comes out of one's most profound sense of being alive. The self-perception, the depth of intuition, the capacity to experience suffering and joy so deeply—for all these reasons poetry speaks out of levels which yield us new truth every time we read it. "Deep calleth unto the deep" describes the experience of being a poet and the reading of poetry.

In the expression of beauty through literature, we also find a basis for reconciliation among nations. In this country we, indeed, hate the very idea of a "police state," as Russia was cruelly called the "evil empire" by President Reagan. But let us not forget that the great contribution of Russia to the world is its surge in the arts in the second half of the nineteenth century. This produced Tolstoy's _War and Peace_, often called the greatest novel ever written and the source of enchantment for millions, plus the amazingly penetrating psychological novels of Dostoyevsky such as _The Brothers Karamazov_, plus the important dramas of Chekhov, which have made such a contribution to the stage. Russia's many other works of literature are paralleled by their musical creativity, which includes Tchaikovsky, Rachmaninoff, Shostakovich and a host of others.

There is surely good reason for the fact that many cultural authorities speak of Russia in the second half of the nineteenth century as the "Second Renaissance," next in importance only to the Italian Renaissance which launched the modern age. We may well, when we are thinking of beauty which transcends all politics and nations, bravely speak of the great arts as the basis for the reconciliation of the warring factions of humankind. In art and poetry and literature there is, to paraphrase St. Paul with a slightly different meaning, "neither male nor female, neither slave nor free, neither Russian nor American."

It is significant that art is the only human institution which is never destructive. Religions turn into wars, as in the Crusades and the endless "holy wars" which continue even in our own day. Economic systems set country against country, as is happening now all over the modern world. But art—not its economic status or prestige status, but *art* itself—is always a win-win situation, the one human institution which never turns persons against persons.

### Will Beauty Save the World?

Dostoyevsky once enigmatically let drop the phrase, "Beauty will save the world." When Solzhenitsyn quoted this in his lecture on receiving the Nobel Prize, he questioned,

> What does this mean? For a long time I thought it merely a phrase. Was such a thing possible? When in our bloodthirsty history did beauty ever save

234

anyone from anything? Ennobled, elevated, yes:
but whom has it saved?

We echo Solzhenitsyn's doubts. Pondering these
doubts, I find myself thinking, "Nothing else seems able
to save us." For no one would be foolish enough to
think that the present policies of the two super-nations
will do any more than produce a stand-off, each with a
revolver at the other's head. We build more nuclear
warheads and the Russians do the same, we invent more
means of destruction and they do the same, each go-
around only repeating the stand-off on a more dangerous scale. Will we still be at the mercy of chance: an
accidental release of some missile, or a terrorist setting
off an atom bomb in New York, and the holocaust will
be upon us? Power, not beauty, seems to govern nations.

What the world can no longer endure in the nuclear
age is its separation into many different nations, each
with its own power needs; and the fact that the United
States seems to be the most powerful is due largely to
the fact that destiny gave us a particularly lush portion
of this globe. But our powerful position should not numb
our realization that we will not be in this position forever. As Athens, at the height of its power and its great,
unrivaled culture, when Aeschylus and Sophocles were
still alive, when Pericles was its leader, when Phidias
had just finished the Parthenon, when Plato was young
and Socrates gathered around him this unequaled group
of young philosophers eternalized in Plato's _Dialogues_—
at its time of glory and power, Athens committed suicide by fighting the Peloponnesian War. Sparta and the
other city-states joined in this useless and wanton sui-

cide. They were all so exhausted by the year 400 B.C. that the days of the city-state were numbered.

We in our twentieth-century world face almost exactly the same challenge. Can we transcend the nation-state? Can we extend our love for country to other countries and the world? Destiny clearly cries out with the challenge to us to extend our imaginations, our economy and our way of thinking, to relate us to the whole planet rather than our own one piece of it.

So long as we view our freedom as dependent upon our remaining the most powerful and richest nation on earth, we shall have placed ourselves again under the sword of Damocles. We shall not be freed from this threat until we confirm a freedom for humanity.

Power brings with it arrogance. Our power in America has brought the arrogance revealed in the remarks that we are the special children of God, we carry His banner, God blesses America and condemns other nations, he has a destiny for us different from that for other nations. Such arrogance, I submit, is radically anti-Christian: It is the Pharisees all over again, "God I thank thee that I am not as other men."

Beauty and power. Were there ever two such strange antagonists? They have almost always been set in opposition to each other, such as Beauty and the Beast. In mythology Beauty is pictured as the radiant but weak maiden, requiring the knight to rescue her from the dark and ugly Power, often pictured as a dragon. How can we be saved by beauty—this gentle but timeless quality, this eternal but ephemeral experience? I recall that as a young boy in winter a snowflake lighted on my black mitten, and just as I was overwhelmed with wonder at its marvelously intricate design, it melted away and left only a wet spot as a token that it was there an instant ago. How can we talk of such a gentle quality saving the world?

Solzhenitsyn reasons that art, and the beauty it expresses, are on a different level from the mundane characteristics of our world.

> There is, however, something special in the essence of beauty, a special quality in art: the conviction carried by a genuine work of art is absolute and subdues even a resistant heart.
>
> A work of art contains its verification in itself. . . . Works which draw on truth and present it to us in live and concentrated form grip us, compellingly involve us, and no one ever, not even ages hence, will come forth to refute them.
>
> Perhaps then the old trinity of Truth, Goodness, and Beauty is not simply the dressed-up, worn-out formula we thought it in our presumptuous, materialistic youth? If the crowns of these three trees meet, as scholars have asserted, and if the too obvious, too straight sprouts of Truth and Goodness have been knocked down, cut off, not let grow, perhaps the whimsical, unpredictable, unexpected branches of Beauty will work their way through, rise up *to that very place*, and thus complete the work of all three?
>
> Then what Dostoyevsky wrote—"Beauty will save the world"—is not a slip of the tongue but a prophecy.

Yes, perhaps. But such an argument, sad to say, sincere and eloquent as it may be, will convince only those who are inclined to believe in the first place. Solzhenitsyn would join us as we try to push beyond this point.

*The Quality of Life*

One thing is certain: a world that does not have a concern for beauty will not be worth saving. Aristotle was surely right when he wrote, "Not life is to be valued, but the *good* life." For all true Greeks, this was central in their concept of *Arētē:* the noble life was first of all the beautiful life.

This is the fundamental importance of beauty and of the art that springs from a love of beauty. The humanities, such as art and music and poetry, exist for one purpose alone: to enhance the quality of human existence. There are riches that lie at hand in any library, waiting to make life fuller, to make us more vital, to disclose to us the presence of joys in life which have been there all the time but we were blind to them. There is no library worth the name which does not have the mental inspiration to take us, like Columbus, to new worlds.

In poetry, in art, in literature, in music, there is not only the power "to tame the savage breast," but to give us the sense of joy and serenity we sorely need. There is music that brings us this with no need for economic riches. Do we need to be awakened to adventure and the sense of passion if our lives are boring? Homer brings us this, as does the poetry in many songs of the Beatles. Taste is a particular approach, but it still can have its value; there is no need to insist that every person experience his soul enlivened by the same things.

Let us have done with the fake serenity that comes from the avoidance of tragedy. We do not need to cite the grandeur of classics like *Hamlet,* but the tragedies

238

which are set in squalor, like O'Neill's _The Ice Man Cometh_, also show us the nobility of the human being. We need not insist that every garden be a rose garden; a meadow with weeds can also be beautiful. There is death as there is life, and let us open ourselves to both. Walter Pater reminds us, "We are all under sentence of death but with a sort of indefinite reprieve; we have an interval, and then our place knows us no more." We affirm life as we affirm death; the two always go together, just as we listen to the discords which play their crucial part in Beethoven's symphonies.

We never have denied that darkness goes with light, or that pain goes with pleasure, and, if the truth were known, makes possible the pleasure, as Plato put it. We have never denied the ugliness that makes beauty possible and necessary, for it is in juxtaposition with ugliness that we are able to recognize beauty.

We can note with pleasure that museums and galleries are becoming increasingly attended these days, and particularly that young people attend more and more exhibitions of art. More people go to galleries than attend football games; and such statistics, absurd on one level, on another tell us that the acquaintanceship with art seems at least to be growing. The galleries and museums give us the presence of adventure and solace, which we, citizens of a technological age, sorely need. Or we can carry with us in memory one picture to give us cheer and purpose, say Botticelli's _Birth of Venus_. Here the faces of Venus and the cherubic spirits of springtime seem woven together by the gossamer breeze, and we are carried away to an Olympus where the gods are not mocked but for once are humble and recognize one of their own.

Beauty is the form which reaches most deeply into

the human heart and mind. It is the language which translates all the moods of humanity into feelings and insights and sensual experience that we can understand. In beauty there are no foreigners: the deeper we penetrate into the human soul, be it of ourselves or our neighbors, the more we find ourselves at one with people of all nations, even those people behind iron curtains. It is by beauty that we feel the pulse of all mankind.

This requires freedom, you say? Yes, freedom of the body within limits, but limits which free the mind. But you may argue, "We have learned in our day to enslave the mind—what do you say to *that?*" The tyranny over the mind we need to fight, but let us make sure what kind of bondage we are fighting, and for what kind of freedom. It is not the freedom to become a millionaire, or the freedom to convince us through clever advertising to buy the million and one things we do not need, nor the things that are deleterious to us. In principle it is the freedom *to be,* not just to possess.

Freedom is indeed an integral part of this beauty, but let it be a genuine freedom, a freedom to think and to feel, a freedom to speak and to contemplate, a freedom to appreciate and to create, a freedom to experience beauty.

Let us return to the major problem of beauty versus power in our world.

For the first time in all human history persons like you and me have been able literally to see the planet in a photograph as a totality. The astronauts, and we through identifying with them and seeing the picture emblazoned in newspapers throughout the world, have

240

been able to gaze at the world as a whirling planet in which all nations now are a part. This photograph is a symbol for a new relationship between nations. We saw the great wall of China, the Indian ocean, the Russian steppes, the north and south Americas, the Atlantic and Pacific oceans. Indeed, in the photograph we were what we in our stubbornness have been trying to escape in reality: all citizens of the same world. In this photograph the Chinese wall shuts out nothing, the perpetual squabbles of the nations turn out to be absurd, the revolvers held at the heads of Russia and the United States are transcended by the spinning planet in its orbit. The whole earth turns slowly before our eyes. I do not mean to belittle our national problems at all: I mean only to present a new symbol of the world which for the first time requires us to see that all countries are citizens of the planet.

Most of all we are grasped in this photograph by how colorful is this new earth, new in the sense that it was our first view of the whole earth. The whirling ball is shimmering gold on the side of the sun, dazzling and resplendent, shading into a brilliant ultramarine. The shadow then merges into inky darkness and on into the pure black of the vast empty corridors that separate us from the solar systems of light far beyond. On and on the blackness stretches to the distant stars.

The photograph was a symbol which can lead us to a radical change in our way of seeing and experiencing the world. The picture reached deeply into my own soul; the nations, usually so noisy, now seemed silent and serene. It showed the nations at last formed into a peaceful co-existence, charmed by the vast spaces of the universe. Can anyone of us let this picture pene-

241

trate into our minds and souls without realizing that we live in a new world, a planet now of a beauty we had not suspected before?

It is not surprising that on Christmas Eve, in the flight of Apollo 8, Captain Frank Borman and his crew of two astronauts read for all the world to hear the story of creation in the book of Genesis. "The earth was without form and void, and darkness was upon the face of the deep. . . . And God said, 'Let there be light.' And God saw that the light was good. . . ." This word "form" from the King James translation has the same meaning as I have used it in describing the form in the work of artists. The "ground forms" Joseph Binder used to emphasize are now wedded to space-forms; we reach not just into our own foundations as Binder taught us, but also into infinity.

One of the astronauts, Russell Schweickart, told me that he carried with him into the stratosphere a number of quotations from different authors, T.S. Eliot, Archibald MacLeish, Gandhi, among them, which he thought might express his experience. One that especially grasped his personal feelings while in orbit was a short poem by Robert Nathan,

> So beauty passes ever out of reach,
> > Save to the heart where happiness is home;
> There beauty walks, wherever it may be,
> > And paints the sunset on a quiet sea.

However we may conceive of the intimations of infinity with which our human minds are endowed, the metaphor of God the Artist is most expressive for many people. That is the concept of the "painter of the sunset on a quiet sea" in Robert Nathan's poem, and includes the forms of the earth as well as of infinity. Form is the essence of all things on heaven and earth, as I have tried to show in many different ways. Its "dwelling is the light of setting suns," in Wordsworth's lines, which I have quoted earlier, "And the round ocean and the living air, . . . A presence that disturbs us with the joy / of elevated thoughts. . . ."

When I asked Russell Schweickart which of his fellow astronauts had uttered the phrase quoted by the newspapers with the photograph of the sun-emblazoned earth, he replied that everyone of them had felt the same thing when they looked out from their spaceship at the whirling earth. It came out in words that one of them suddenly exclaimed,

"God, it's beautiful!"

# ACKNOWLEDGEMENTS

It is a pleasure to mention some persons who have discussed with me this work as it was in progress. Richard Wiseman, who has been amazingly rich in references, I often call the librarian of the soul. There are also Georgia Johnson, Magda Denes, Don Michael, Jay Oglvy, and Peter Koestenbaum. My secretary Paula Raskin, an artist in her own right, did the drawing on page 47, the only one in the book for which I cannot claim authorship. Don May, the designer of this book, and the staff of Saybrook Publishing Company have been of indispensable help in this project. One feels a certain familyship with those with whom one has shared ideas as they are formulated.

The lines from Wallace Stevens's Poem "Sunday Morning," on pages 67 and 71, are quoted from *The Collected Poems of Wallace Stevens*, reprinted by permission of Alfred A. Knopf, Inc. Copyright (c) 1954 by Wallace Stevens.